IRELAND

IRELAND

SOME EPISODES FROM HER PAST

by Howard Smith

BRITISH BROADCASTING CORPORATION

The television series *Ireland: some episodes from her past*
is rebroadcast on BBC 1 from April to June 1974.

Published to accompany a series of programmes
prepared in consultation with the BBC Further
Education Advisory Council

© Howard Smith
and the British Broadcasting Corporation 1974
First Published 1974
Published by the British Broadcasting Corporation
35 Marylebone High Street, London W1M 4AA

Printed in England by Jolly and Barber Ltd, Rugby
ISBN: 0 563 10785 5

CONTENTS

Acknowledgment is due to the following for permission to reproduce illustrations:

BELFAST TELEGRAPH page 64 (top); BODLEIAN LIBRARY, OXFORD page 10; THE TRUSTEES OF THE BRITISH MUSEUM pages 49 (both), 52 (both) and 53 (all); J. CASHMAN pages 80 (both) and 81 (bottom); CONSERVATIVE PARTY RESEARCH DEPARTMENT page 55 (bottom); IRISH TIMES page 91; MANSELL COLLECTION page 56; G. MORRISON page 31 (both); NATIONAL GALLERY OF IRELAND, DUBLIN pages 17 (both), 116 (both), and 117 (all); NATIONAL LIBRARY OF IRELAND, DUBLIN pages 30 (both), 73 (both), 78 (bottom), 79 (both), and 81 (top); NATIONAL MUSEUM OF IRELAND, DUBLIN pages 71 (all), 72 (all), 74 and 82 (top); NATIONAL PORTRAIT GALLERY, LONDON page 42; PUBLIC RECORD OFFICE OF NORTHERN IRELAND pages 54 (top right and bottom right) and 59; RADIO TIMES HULTON PICTURE LIBRARY pages 50 (both), 51 (both), 82 (bottom) and 85 (both); REFORM CLUB, LONDON page 33; TOPIX page 78 (top); ULSTER FOLK MUSEUM page 111 (top); ULSTER MUSEUM pages 54 (top left and bottom left), 55 (top), 61, 63 (top), 64, 65 (both), 66 (all) and 113 (bottom); WELCH COLLECTION, ULSTER MUSEUM pages 63 (bottom), 110 (both), 111 (bottom), 112 (both) and 113 (top).

The photographs on pages 54, 55, 59, 61, 63 (top), 64, 65 and 66 were taken by Jim Bennett, and those on pages 49, 52 and 53 by Roynon Raikes.

Acknowledgment is also due to:

CONTROLLER, STATIONERY OFFICE, DUBLIN for map on page 120 based on one in *The Restoration of the Irish Language* published 1965 and for table on page 26 from *The Report of the Commission on Emigration* published 1956; maps on pages 90 (right) and 95 based on documents from Public Record Office, London. Crown copyright reserved; FABER AND FABER LTD for map on page 14 based on one from *The Williamite Confiscation in Ireland 1690-1703*; MRS KATHERINE KAVANAGH for extract on page 29 from *The Great Hunger* by Patrick Kavanagh, published by Macgibbon & Kee 1966; map on page 90 (left) based on one from the *Morning Post* 7.11.25; map on page 47 is taken from *The Distribution and Segregation of Roman Catholics in Belfast* by Emrys Jones which was first published in THE SOCIOLOGICAL REVIEW, Vol. 4, 1956.

The maps were drawn by Brian and Constance Dear.

INTRODUCTION

'It all goes back', said the white-haired Nationalist veteran, smiling his grim smile, 'to March 29th 1613.' Now it happens that March 29th is my birthday; otherwise I think it is highly unlikely that I should have remembered the date (which I happened to have read only a few days before) and been able to reply: 'Yes, of course; that was when the county of Londonderry was created'.

It brought home to me, however, more forcibly than almost anything else, something that many other people have said to me, both before and since – and which indeed has become something of a truism: that there is nowhere else in the world where what happened in the past (and often a long time in the past) is still so important to people today as Ireland. In England we *accept* our history. We may approve or disapprove of particular actions in the past; we may approve or disapprove of their continuing effects. But, in general, whether we approve or disapprove, we take the view that what's done is done, that we must take things as we find them. But the Irishman's attitude is different, simply because there are many issues in Irish history that have not reached the stage of finality that the Englishman takes for granted. Two such issues – which are closely related – are still important. One is the relationship between Ireland and England; the other is the relationship between the two sections of the Irish population. And the two issues are so closely connected because the minority group in Ireland has generally relied on English support.

It is because these issues are still alive that history plays such a large part in Irish politics. The fight is still on; and history is treated as wartime propaganda. People feel obliged to justify what 'their side' did in the past: and they find in the actions of the 'other side' (perhaps centuries ago) grounds for their own attitudes and policies. These conflicting interpretations of the past are perhaps symptoms rather than causes of the present division between the two groups in Ireland. But to realise that they exist is a necessary step towards understanding the situation today.

In December 1971 I started work on a series of television programmes which attempted to explain the background to the current situation in both Northern Ireland and the Republic through an analysis of the island's past. This book develops the themes covered in those ten programmes. It is not a comprehensive history of Ireland; it concentrates rather on those events, movements and personalities in the past which still have some influence today. It is intended for those who have no previous knowledge of Irish history, but who would like to feel that at least they can understand the background to the present conflict, whatever they may feel about the possibility of its eventual resolution.

This book is not, I ought to add, particularly original. It is based, first of all, on the detailed briefs prepared for the television series by Professor F. S. L. Lyons. I am especially grateful to him, both for such a stimulating introduction to the subject, and for his constant help and encouragement both with the television programmes and with the manuscript of the book. I am also grateful to Professor J. C. Beckett and to Professor Oliver MacDonagh, who read both the scripts of the television programmes and the manuscript of this book, and who made a multitude of helpful comments and suggestions. I would also like to thank all those who helped me with the preparation of the television programmes, especially Brigit Barry, Giles Oakley and Rod Smith; and my assistant, Vera Philip, who has typed considerably more pages on the subject than either she, or I, ever expected.

HOWARD SMITH

DONEGAL

LONDONDERRY
• Londonderry

ANTRIM
Larne •

Castledawson •

TYRONE

Belfast

R Lagan
Donaghadee •
Bangor

DOWN

LEITRIM

FERMANAGH
Enniskillen •

Armagh •

ARMAGH

Clones
MONAGHAN

SLIGO

CAVAN

LOUTH

MAYO
Westport •

• Ballaghadereen
ROSCOMMON

LONGFORD

Battle of the
Boyne·1690
Drogheda •

MEATH

Balbriggan •

Westport •

WESTMEATH

R. Boyne

Clontarf

GALWAY
Galway •

OFFALY*

Prosperous •
• Bodenstown

Howth •

Dublin
DUBLIN

Aran
Islands

R. Shannon

LEIX*

KILDARE

Kilcoole •

WICKLOW

CLARE
• Ennis

Woodenbridge •

CARLOW

Limerick •

TIPPERARY

Kilkenny •
KILKENNY

LIMERICK

• Cashel

WEXFORD

Wexford •

KERRY

CORK

WATERFORD

Waterford •

Cork •

*Offaly was formerly known as King's County
and Leix as Queen's County.

REMEMBER 1690!

When, in August 1969, the full significance of the crisis in Northern Ireland finally burst on a startled British public, few of those who recoiled from the grim reality on their television screens knew why the eruption had taken place. Fewer still knew that 1969 was the 800th anniversary of England's first involvement in Ireland.

For it was indeed in May 1169 that a small force from the Welsh marches led by Robert FitzStephen landed in Ireland. They were followed the next year by another force led by Richard de Clare, Earl of Pembroke – better known as Strongbow. They had come at the invitation of Dermot MacMurrough, King of Leinster. Dermot had done homage to King Henry II of England and in return had given Dermot permission to seek English allies in his struggle against his Irish enemies. The Norman invasion of Ireland was so successful that in 1171 Henry II, fearing the establishment of a powerful independent Kingdom, himself came to Ireland and secured the submission of his own barons and many of the Irish kings to himself as Lord of Ireland. It also seems likely (though there is no direct evidence for it) that the English conquest of Ireland had been sanctioned by the Pope.

During the next 75 years the Norman invaders succeeded in establishing their authority over a large part of the country. There was no overall plan of conquest. The Normans were successful because their weapons, their tactics and their military discipline were so much better than those of the native Irish. By the end of the thirteenth century however the native Irish had begun to win back much of the territory they had lost, and by the middle of the fifteenth century the English royal authority in Ireland had shrunk to a small area round Dublin known as the Pale.

There were two main reasons for this. In the first place, for most of the 350 years after Henry II's visit in 1171 the Kings of England were too far away and too concerned with events either in England or in France to be able to consolidate their authority in Ireland. In the second place, there were too few Normans in Ireland to absorb, or even to dominate, the native Irish. The Normans therefore had a recurring tendency to go native, and to become, in the contemporary phrase, *Hibernis ipsis hiberniores* – more Irish than the Irish. As the Statute of Kilkenny complained in 1366:

'Now many English of the said land, forsaking the English language, fashion, manner of riding, laws and customs, live and govern themselves by the manners, fashion and language of the Irish enemies, and have made many marriages and alliances between themselves and the Irish enemies, by which the said land and its liege people, the English language, the allegiance due to our lord the King and the English laws are put in subjection and decayed and the Irish enemies raised up.'

For this reason the King's government in London preferred increasingly to rely on the 'English born in England' to govern what was left of their Irish territories. But by the time Henry Tudor came to the throne in 1485, the English crown no longer had either the financial or the military resources to enforce English rule through Englishmen. By then, too, one of the leading families of the 'English born in Ireland', the Fitzgeralds of Kildare, had managed – by marrying into the native aristocracy – to establish themselves as a considerable power both inside and outside the Pale. The Earls of Kildare, it was decided in London, would be a more efficient instrument of the royal power than any man sent from England. For nearly fifty years the Fitzgeralds governed Ireland for the English crown as Lords Deputy.

But this system of indirect rule was unsatisfactory, especially for the ambitious Henry VIII. In 1534, after several attempts had been made to weaken his authority, Kildare rebelled against the English crown. The rebellion was defeated and in 1541 Henry was declared King of Ireland. The change was underlined by the introduction of a new policy of surrender and re-grant: the leading families – English and Irish – surrendered their land to the crown and were granted it back again as the crown's subjects. However, this assertion of English royal authority over Ireland ignored the fact that in Irish law eldest sons did not inherit all their

Perhaps the earliest example of a well-known English stereotype. Two Irishmen fighting, from an early thirteenth century manuscript of Giraldus Cambrensis' Typographia Hibernia.

father's land, and that chiefs were elected by their clans. In such a society, the only permanent settlement would be one made by conquest. Without such a conquest, the assertion of English royal authority remained an assertion and could never become a reality.

The inherent instability of this new arrangement was emphasised by the Protestant Reformation. As long as this meant simply Henry VIII's breach with the Pope's authority in Rome, the Irish accepted it. But the fundamental religious changes that followed under Edward VI – the celebration of the Mass, for example, was made illegal – were strongly resented by both Irish and English, and they refused to accept them. Many of these changes were confirmed by the religious settlement of Elizabeth I, but both Irish and English in Ireland still refused to accept the Reformation. As England became more and more involved in the religious wars of the later sixteenth century, and especially after Elizabeth was excommunicated by the Pope in 1580, Ireland became a potential base for England's Catholic enemies – especially Spain. The conquest of Ireland therefore became an indispensable element in English policy. And so there began that fatal intermingling of race, politics and religion which has influenced Irish history ever since.

Elizabeth's Irish wars dragged on intermittently from 1569 to 1603, a constant drain on the country's finances, and a continual challenge to the troops morale. 'When they are weary with wars and brought down to extreme wretchedness', wrote Edmund Spenser of his Irish opponents, 'then they creep a little perhaps and sue for grace, till they have gotten new breath and recovered strength again. So it is in vain to speak of planting of laws and plotting of policies till they be altogether subdued.'

The last and most serious challenge to English rule was the rebellion of Hugh O'Neill, Earl of Tyrone, in Ulster. But what in its earlier stages had threatened to become a country-wide rising with Spanish assistance was finally broken in March 1603. Although both O'Neill and his fellow rebel, Hugh O'Donnell, Earl of Tyrconnell, were given generous terms, both

quickly realised that military defeat was to be followed by a conscious and deliberate attempt to destroy the native Irish social and political system – which the Elizabethans regarded as anarchic and barbarous. In 1607 the Earls left Ireland for Spain.

Already before this 'flight of the Earls' much had been done to introduce English landowners, English institutions and the Anglican church into Ulster – 'the most rude and unreformed part of Ireland and the seat and nest of the last great rebellion'. With the Earls' departure the removal of 'barbarism' and 'superstition' and its replacement by 'civility' and 'religion' could be more systematic. In the previous century several attempts had been made to plant loyal English settlers on Irish land, but these plantations were largely swept away in Elizabeth's Irish wars. Now an attempt was made to achieve a 'positive reformation by plantation' in Ulster on the lands confiscated from the earls, to expel many of the native Irish, and to introduce an English colony large enough and powerful enough to keep the peace.

In 1609 great areas of these lands – re-organised as the counties of Armagh, Cavan, Coleraine, Donegal, Fermanagh and Tyrone – were accordingly granted out to 'undertakers' on condition that they planted their estates with English and Scottish settlers, and to 'servitors' who were allowed to take Irish tenants. The county of Coleraine was planted by the twelve great livery companies of London and changed its name to Londonderry. At the same time the counties of Antrim and Down were similarly planted, notably by Scots like Henry Montgomery and James Hamilton in north Down, and these plantations also attracted considerable numbers of Scots. All the new settlers were Protestants, and most of the Scots were Presbyterians. Though the Presbyterians did not spread far outside the north-east, the Ulster Plantation introduced a third religious group into the country which has lasted ever since.

From the English point of view, the plantation of Ulster was far from satisfactory. In the first place, contrary to the government's intention, there was no whole-

Page 12: two illustrations from John Derrick's Image of Irlande, published in 1581. The first shows the kind of activity common in a society dominated by tribal feuds, where cattle were the main symbol of wealth; the other (below) is a Protestant comment on the activities of Catholic priests. In 1580 Pope Gregory XIII granted a plenary indulgence to all who took up arms against Queen Elizabeth I.
Page 13: this religious sanction for attacks on Protestants is taken up in one (marked R) of a series of atrocities vividly described in a contemporary account of the Ulster Rebellion of 1641.

sale removal of the Irish; many indeed were kept on as tenants on land they had once owned. But not only were the Irish not removed, they remained in the majority – with consequences graphically described in an early report on the Londonderry plantation:

'This plantation already done is to small purpose without another plantation further into the country, and British sent over, which would prevent many robberies and murders daily committed by the Irish, to the great terror of the few poor British already planted, many of them having lost all they had.'

In 1641 the native Irish in the north rebelled in an attempt to recover the lands they had lost in the plantation. The Ulster rebellion was accompanied by considerable brutality and this was magnified in popular propaganda into a concerted plan to massacre the entire Protestant population. Eight years later when Oliver Cromwell, having won the English civil war and seen Charles I executed, came to subdue Ireland, the imagined scale of the atrocities supposed to have been committed in 1641 was largely responsible for his massacre of the garrison at Drogheda. 'I am persuaded', said Cromwell, 'that this is a righteous judgement of God upon these barbarous wretches, who have imbrued their hands in innocent blood.'

Cromwell's decisive campaign in Ireland was followed by an equally decisive expropriation of Catholic landlords and their replacement by Protestants. Many of those who lost their land this time were the older English families – the 'English born in Ireland' who remained loyal both to the Roman Catholic church and to the British crown – until in 1641 they had thrown in their lot with the native Irish. The wholesale transfer of land that took place in the 1650s increased the proportion in Protestant hands from about 40 per cent to about 75 per cent of the total, and as a consequence the balance of political power in Ireland – which was based on land – shifted equally decisively to the Protestants. But though the ownership of land changed hands, tenancy – as in Ulster – very often did not. The result was to create a thinly spread Protestant ruling class over an embittered, dispossessed, but still *present* Catholic population – in the words of a contemporary: 'The old proprietors who evermore haunt and live about those lands whereof they were dispossessed and cannot forbear to hope and reckon a day of repossession'.

A few of the former owners got their land back again at the Restoration of Charles II in 1660. For the rest, the existence of a restless and potentially violent majority, and the memory – real or imagined – of the 1641 rebellion, meant that Protestant landowners still feared that they might lose both their land and their lives. These fears were intensified first by Charles II's disposition to tolerate Catholics, and then in 1685 by the succession of James II, an acknowledged Catholic, to the British throne. James's Lord Lieutenant in Ireland, Richard Talbot, Earl of Tyrconnell, embarked on a determined programme of restoring power to the Catholics. Fearing what would almost certainly have followed if Tyrconnell had been allowed to complete this programme – the reversal of Cromwell's land settlement – many Protestants sold up and crossed to England where they helped to swell the growing opposition to James II.

James left England in December 1688. In March 1689, a month after he had been deposed by the British parliament and the crown offered to William of Orange, James landed in Ireland, which had remained loyal to the Stuarts. For the next two years the battle for supremacy in the British Isles (and with it an important campaign in the European war between Louis XIV of France and a coalition of smaller powers) was fought out in Ireland. The war gave Irish Protestants two of their most sacred symbols – the relief of Londonderry after fifteen weeks siege in 1689, and the battle of the Boyne on 1 July 1690.[1]

Though the war dragged on until the following summer, William's defeat of James II at the Boyne was as decisive as its continuing fame suggests; it decided that a Protestant minority would rule in Ireland. William's

[1] When, during the eighteenth century, the calendar was reformed, 1 July became 12 July, the day on which the battle is commemorated.

A Here creepes out of Sainct Filchers denne, a packe of prowling mates,
   Most hurtfull to the Gnglish pale, and noysome to the states:
   Which spare no moze their country bypth, then those of th'english race,
   But yeld to each a lyke good turne, when as they come in place.
B They spoyle, and burne, and beare away, as fitte occasions serue,
   And thinke the greater ill they doe, the greater prayse deserue:

2 They passe not for the poore mans cry, nor yet respect his teares,
   But rather ioy to see the fire, to flash about his eares.
   To see both flame, and smouldring smoke, to duske the chriftall skyes,
   Next to their pray, therein I say, their second glory lyes.
C And thus bereauing him of house, of cattell and of stoze:
   They do returne backe to the wooo, from whence they came befoze.

   And when with myzth and belly cheere, they are sufficed well,
   Marke what ensueth, a playne discourse, of Jrish sleightes J tell:
A The Fryer then absolues the theefe, from all his former sinne.
   And bids him plague the princes frendes, if heauen he minde to winne.
B Which being sayd, he takes his hozse, to put in practise then,
   The spoyling and destroying of, her graces loyall men.

4 C But Loe the souldiers then the plague, vnto this Karnish rowt:
      To yeldthem vengaunce for their sinnes, in warlicke sort rise out.
      They preffe the rancoure of the theeues, by force of bloudy knife.
      And stay the pray they filcht away, depriuing them of life:
   D The Fryer then that traytrous knaue, with Ough Ough hone lament:
      To see his coosin Deuills sonnes, to haue so fowle euent.

At one Mr Atkins house 7 Papyftes brake in & beate
out his braines. then riped upe his Wife with childe
after they had rauished her & Nero like vewed natu
res bed of conception then tooke they the Childe
and facrificed it in the fire

English Proteftantes ftriped naked & turned into
the mountaines in the froft, & fnowe, whereof many
hundreds are perifhed to death. & many lynge
dead in diches & Sauages upbraided them faynge.
now are ye wilde Irifh as well as wee.

Driuinge Men women & children by hund:
reds upon Briges & cafting them into Riuers,
who drowned not were killed with poles &
fhot with muffets.

Mr Daucnant and his Wife bound in their
Chaires ftriped the 2 Eldeft Children of 7
yeares old rofted upon Spittes before their
Parents faces Cutt their throte and after
murdred him.

The Preeftes & Iefuites anoite the Rebells with
there Sacrament of vnction before they go to
murther & robe aſſuringe them that for there
meritorious Seruice if they be killed he fhall
efcape Purgatory & go to heauen immediatly.

Pulling them about the ftreetes by the haire of
the head, dafhing the Childrens braines againft
the poftes faynge. these were the pigges of
the English Sowes.

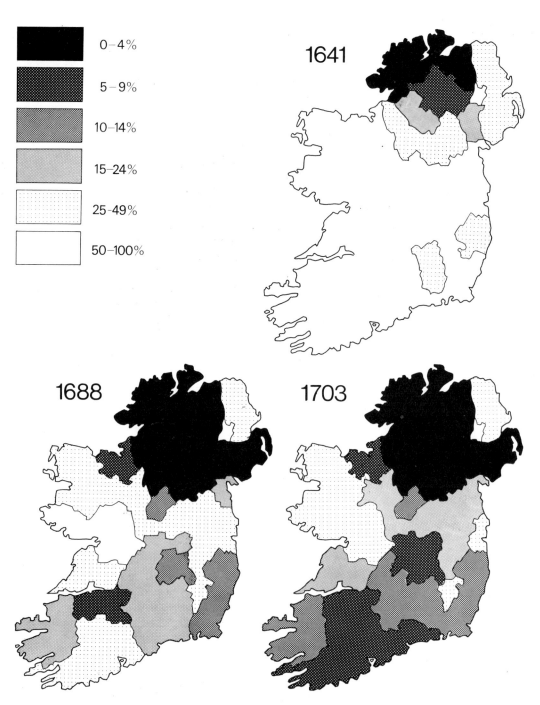

0–4%

5–9%

10–14%

15–24%

25–49%

50–100%

1641

1688

1703

victory had two major consequences. First, there was another transfer of land from Catholics to Protestants. In 1688 Protestants had owned 78 per cent of all Irish land; by 1709 they owned 86 per cent. Second, the Protestant minority set out to protect itself once and for all from the Catholic majority and to prevent Catholics from ever again threatening the Protestants special position.

The original intention was to make the practice of Catholicism impossible. In practice however bishops continued to be appointed, the numbers of clergy increased, schools were held, churches built, baptisms, marriages and burials continued. In any case the attempt to extinguish the Catholic religion was less significant to Protestants than their determination to keep the Catholic population in a position of permanent social, economic and political inferiority. Here the series of penal laws, passed between 1692 and 1709, was considerably more successful. Catholics were forbidden to carry arms, they were excluded from all government offices, they could not hold commissions in the army or navy, they could not enter the legal profession, and they were forbidden to buy land or to hold it on lease for more than 31 years.[2]

Even here, however, it proved impossible to enforce the penal laws with the full rigour that had been intended. As the years passed, and the Catholic danger receded, Protestants were less and less inclined to enforce them at all. Many Catholics managed to climb the ladder of economic advancement, especially in trade and industry, and after 1750 this gave them increasing social and political influence. But the majority of the population – as in every other European country – remained poor, and as liable as ever to react in wild outbursts of agrarian violence. But though in Ireland this population was almost exclusively Catholic, violence was always caused by economic grievances and was never consciously motivated by a feeling of religious persecution.

In Ulster the existence of a substantial Protestant population meant that there was generally a happier relationship between landlord and tenant than in the rest of the country. This led to the growth of the so-called Ulster Custom, which gave tenants some protection against eviction and some guarantee that they would not lose the benefit of any improvement they might make to their holdings. Ulster was also the centre of the new and growing linen industry. The industry was based largely in the countryside, with the spinning and weaving of cloth being carried on by individuals in their own cottages. The effects were frequently noticed by visitors – by John Wesley, for example, in 1756: 'No sooner did we enter Ulster than we observed the difference. The ground was cultivated just as in England, and the cottages not only neat, but with doors, chimneys and windows'.

Those who benefited most from the growth of the linen industry were the bleachers and drapers who bought the unfinished cloth. Many became wealthy and influential and this led, especially in Belfast, to the emergence of a new commercial middle class – comfortable, well-educated and independent-minded – and strong enough by 1786 to bypass Dublin and establish their own marketing organisation. Many were Presbyterians, but though their prosperity gave them social and political influence, Presbyterians lacked the political power which their social position would normally have given them. For although Catholics were the main victims of the penal laws, they were not the only ones. The Presbyterians of the north-east were also excluded by law from all offices of civil and military employment under the crown and from membership of municipal corporations – and this was especially significant in towns like Belfast and Londonderry, which had been virtually created by Presbyterian enterprise.

Their exclusion was due partly to the fact that already by 1690 the Presbyterians were a large, well-organised and articulate minority who could threaten the privileged position of the landed gentry. But it was also caused by genuine religious feeling. Presbyterians despised members of the established church, which they regarded as 'no better if not worse than popery itself'.

[2] In 1728 Catholics were also formally deprived of the vote.

Anglicans hated Presbyterians because of the democratic, anti-authoritarian nature of their church, a feeling described with characteristic venom by Jonathan Swift:

And thus Fanatic Saints tho' neither in
Doctrine or Discipline our Brethren
Are Brother Protestants and Christians
As much as Hebrews and Philistines
But in no other sense than Nature
Has made a Rat our Fellow Creature.

In spite of the numbers and significance of the Presbyterian minority, this minority could be discriminated against because 'in cases of public danger and invasion all people were obliged both in duty and interest to oppose the common enemy' – in other words, in any emergency Presbyterians were bound to side with Anglicans against the common Catholic danger.

The main effect of the Williamite settlement of the 1690s in fact had been to put the government of Ireland in the hands of a small class of landowners, who were also members of the established-Anglican-church of Ireland, and who (through their virtual monopoly of the seats) dominated the Irish Parliament in Dublin which watched over their interests. It was this Anglo-Irish Protestant Ascendancy who dotted the countryside with their splendid houses and who made Dublin the second city of the Empire where, said a contemporary: 'Society in the upper classes was as brilliant and polished as that of Paris in its best days'.

On the surface this Protestant Ascendancy seemed secure enough. But it was vulnerable not only because it was based on the exclusion from power of both Catholics and Presbyterians, but also because its freedom of action was severely limited. Although Ireland had her own Parliament, the men who actually governed Ireland – the Lord Lieutenant and his officials in Dublin Castle – were appointed by the British crown. Their major concern was to manage the Irish parliament so that the rivalries and alliances of its members could be harnessed to carrying on the policy of the British government at Westminster. Moreover, though the Irish Parliament could in principle legislate for Irish matters, in practice its power to do so was extremely limited. Poynings Law of 1494 prevented it from initiating legislation without British approval, and by an Act of 1719 (known as the Sixth of George 1st) the British Parliament had declared its right to legislate for Ireland without reference to the Dublin Parliament.

Throughout the eighteenth century there were nationalist stirrings among the gentry in the Irish Parliament against their continued subordination to Westminster but it was not until the 1770s that a 'patriotic' opposition began to assume any coherence. When the American war of independence broke out in 1775 however, it was widely recognised in Ireland that the American colonists were fighting for the same kind of independence from Westminster as the 'patriots' themselves claimed for Ireland. When practically all the British troops in Ireland were withdrawn to fight in the American colonies, and when both France and Spain entered the war on the American side, Ireland lay open to invasion. First in Belfast, and then all over the country Irish Protestants – Catholics were still not allowed to bear arms – formed Volunteer Corps, and by the middle of 1779 a Volunteer army had sprung into existence. But it was an army under the control not of the government, but of the politically aware minority – and even more important, one which included large numbers of those then excluded from political power – the Presbyterians.

The Volunteers had been formed to resist the French, 'the jealous enemies of our liberties and our religion', but they provided a new and significant focus for Irish resentment of British control. As a contemporary complained: 'Under pretence of preparing an invasion on this island, all sorts of Protestants, but the Dissenters most warmly, have taken up arms, which they now threaten to employ against England'. Using the military strength of the Volunteers as a threat, the 'patriot' group in the Irish Parliament, led by Henry Grattan, was able to force the British government to make concessions. In 1779 most of the restrictions on Irish trade

Left: Henry Grattan
Right: Wolfe Tone

imposed by the British Parliament (which were seen at the time as the major barrier to Irish prosperity) were removed. It proved more difficult to establish the exclusive right of the Irish Parliament to legislate for Irish affairs and even to get a majority for such a declaration in the Irish Parliament. In May 1782, however, after a change of administration in London, the British government agreed to repeal the Sixth of George 1st and to amend Poynings Law; the British crown abandoned the right to initiate legislation in the Irish Parliament, but retained the right of veto.

But the winning of the so-called 'Constitution of 1782' was a hollow victory. The Irish government was still run by the Lord Lieutenant, and the Lord Lieutenant was appointed on the advice of the British government. The final authority in fact remained, as it had always remained, in London.

And there was a fundamental split in the patriots' ranks about what they were to *do* with their new-found legislative independence. From the start there was friction between those – mainly the landed gentry – who believed that the 'Constitution of 1782' had been won for the privileged minority in the Irish Parliament, and the radicals – mainly middle-class Protestants, especially northern Presbyterians – who believed that the Irish Parliament should be reformed and that they should share power with the privileged minority. Parliament was *not* reformed, power was *not* shared and the political aspirations of the excluded radicals remained unsatisfied.

More important than this was the fundamental disagreement over the repeal of the penal laws and the restoration of equal rights to the Catholics – Catholic Emancipation. Most Protestants by now found the penal laws distasteful and few doubted that they should be relaxed; what was at issue was how far this relaxation should go. 'So long as we exclude Catholics from natural liberty and the common rights of man we are not a people' said the radical Henry Grattan. 'I admit the merit of the Roman Catholics and that merit makes me consent to enlarge their privileges', said the conservative Henry Flood, 'but I will not consent to

their having any influence in choosing members for this House'. Even liberals were confused about the granting of *political* rights. 'To extend the right of suffrage to our Roman Catholic brethren', ran a resolution of the 1784 Volunteer Convention, 'still preserving in its fullest extent the present Protestant government'. Though radicals continued to press for Catholic emancipation, it was the British government, anxious to reduce potential sources of trouble, who made the running. They had already in 1779 passed a law allowing Catholics to lease land in perpetuity. Once started it became impossible to stop the movement towards complete reform. Further measures of relief followed in 1782 and 1792, and in 1793 Catholics were finally given the vote – though they could still not sit in Parliament.

But what did most to undermine the precarious equilibrium of 1782 was the French Revolution. When the Revolution broke out, in 1789, it was widely welcomed, but when it moved from constitutional reform to violence – and especially when Louis XVI and Marie Antoinette were guillotined in 1793 – there was a profound revulsion of feeling among the leading members of the Ascendancy. Whilst the elite became more than ever determined to defend the status quo, the more radical Protestants moved closer to the democratic ideas of the French Revolution. In 1791, in Belfast, they founded the Society of United Irishmen, whose aim, as the name implies, was to bring all Irishmen together in pursuit of liberty. Or, in the famous words of one of their founders, Wolfe Tone: 'To subvert the tyranny of our execrable government, to break the connection with England (the never-failing source of all our political evils) and to assert the independence of my country – these were my objects. To unite the whole people of Ireland; to abolish the memory of all past dissensions; and to substitute the common name of Irishman in place of the denominations of Protestant, Catholic and Dissenter – these were my means'.

By 1793 Britain and France were at war, the majority of the Protestant Ascendancy in Ireland retreated still further into rigid conservatism, and every attempt at constitutional reform was defeated in the Irish parliament. The United Irishmen came to believe that the only policy open to them was to destroy the system and the only method rebellion – if necessary with French assistance.

The Protestant elite had resisted radical demands for reform largely because they feared that democratic ideas would inflame the Catholic peasantry to rebellion. French influence was blamed for the increase in agrarian outrages that occurred in the 1790s. But this was in fact due not so much to French influence, as to the economic pressures of a rapidly increasing population competing for land. There had also been increasing friction in the North between Protestant and Catholic tenants, but the competition now became acute as more and more Protestants found themselves outbid for new tenancies by Catholics who were prepared to accept a lower standard of living. The situation rapidly deteriorated into almost continuous local warfare between rival gangs of Protestants – Peep O'Day Boys – and Catholics – Defenders. In 1795 this led to the establishment of the Orange Society (later the Orange Order) by Protestants in Co. Armagh to protect the interests of Protestant farmers. The Catholics responded by joining the Defenders in even greater numbers.

The United Irishmen were essentially a small group of middle-class urban intellectuals with little understanding of – or sympathy for – the plight of Catholic peasants. Their leaders, however, were quick to see the revolutionary potential of the Defenders. In the North, where the United Irishmen were best organised, they began to arm the peasants with pikes and muskets. The government were equally aware of the potential danger and in 1797 General Lake was sent to Belfast to 'pacify' the north. The campaign of unrestrained and brutal repression which followed guaranteed that only a small and dedicated minority would continue to plan a rebellion.

When the rebellion finally did come in 1798, it was desperate, sporadic and un-coordinated. In Ulster, where the idealism of the United Irishmen still flickered, a largely Protestant rising was quickly crushed. Farther south in Co. Wexford, a rising of Catholic peasantry, in which many priests took an active part, lasted rather longer and was distinguished by considerable and indiscriminate brutality on both sides before, during and after the rising. Far from being the champions of national freedom that they became in later legend, however, the 'boys of Wexford' were motivated by the local grievances of an oppressed peasantry, and not by the ideas of Wolfe Tone and the Belfast radicals.

The rebellion might have stood some chance of success if it had coincided with a French invasion, which was something Wolfe Tone had spent several years in France trying to achieve. In 1796 he had seen one expedition dispersed by a storm and by disagreement amongst its commanders. In 1798 the French changed their plans and replaced a full-scale invasion with several smaller operations. Tone came with one which was intercepted off Donegal. He was captured, sentenced to death and committed suicide in prison.

Although superior British forces eventually crushed the rising of 1798, nothing could disguise the fact that, at a time of great crisis, Ireland had been exposed as a dangerous weakness in British defences. The British government argued that the Protestant Ascendancy could only be secured by a union of the two countries in which the Protestants would always be in a permanent majority. Or, as Lord Clare put it rather more dramatically in the Irish Parliament: 'The whole power and property [of Ireland] has been conferred by successive monarchs of England upon an English colony composed of three sets of English adventurers who poured into this country at the termination of three successive rebellions. Confiscation is their common title and from their first settlement they have been hemmed in on every side by the old inhabitants of this island, brooding over their discontents in sullen indignation. What was the security of the English settlers for their physical existence [in 1691]? And what is the security of their descendants at this day? The powerful and commanding position of Great Britain. If, by any fatality, it fails, you are at the mercy of the old inhabitants of this island, and I should have hoped that the samples of mercy

Two engravings attacking British behaviour during the 1798 rebellion, published in Watty Cox's Irish Magazine *in 1810* – Captain Swayne pitch-capping the people of Prosperous *(top) and* Plan of a travelling gallows used in 1798 *(bottom). There are two more examples of this spirited anti-British propaganda on the next page.*

exhibited by them in the progress of the late rebellion, would have taught the gentlemen who call themselves the Irish nation to reflect with sober attention on the dangers which surround them'.

The Ascendancy had indeed been badly shaken by the violence and bitterness of the rebellion, and by the twin spectres of popery and democracy it had raised. Many had also become thoroughly disillusioned by the failure of the 1782 Constitution; the fragile demonstration of patriotic unity had long been shattered by the controversies over parliamentary reform and Catholic Emancipation. Many were still reluctant to give up their limited independence, fearing that their interests would be submerged by a Union, and many had to be compensated for the loss of their parliamentary seats.[3]

In the end the Irish Parliament was won over not, as was once thought, by bribery and corruption, but by the reluctant recognition that union was the least undesirable alternative. An Act of Union was passed by both the British and the Irish Parliaments. The Irish Parliament was abolished, and on January 1st 1801 Ireland was merged with Great Britain in the United Kingdom.

[3] William Pitt, the British Prime Minister, had originally intended that Union should be accompanied by Catholic Emancipation; some of the opposition to Union almost certainly arose from the fear that this would weaken the Protestant ascendancy (see chapter 3, page 32).

Top: Lord A going out in the morning. *Notice the triangle – much used in the early stages of the 1798 rebellion – to which men were tied to be flogged with the cat o' nine tails – also prominently displayed.* Bottom: The gun beggars of Clones *is an attack on the activities of the Orange Order in the early nineteenth century.*

Right: two of George Cruickshanks' engravings for W H Maxwell's History of the Irish Rebellion of 1798, *first published in 1845 –* Rebels executing prisoners on Wexford Bridge *(top) and* Carousal and plunder in the Bishop of Ferns' palace *(bottom).*

THE LAND FOR THE PEOPLE

'A disaster so appalling that no words can sum its tragedy.'

'The most terrible of all the terrible disasters in Irish history.'

'One of those events which come now and then to do the work of ages in a day and to change the very nature of an entire society.'

Historians are agreed about the crucial significance of the great famine of the 1840s; indeed its significance was clear even to contemporaries. Its greatest effect was undoubtedly psychological – the Irish had always hated the English for taking over their country, for displacing them from ownership of the land and reducing them to the status of tenants and labourers. Now they held the English responsible for the scale and horror of the disaster that overtook them. Some even accused the English of a deliberate intention to exterminate the Irish.

But the famine had more tangible results which were equally important. It led to the mass emigration of millions of Irish overseas, especially to the United States, and this in turn transformed the Irish question into an international problem. It also led to a sudden and dramatic fall in the population, which then continued to fall for a further hundred years, a fall which has only recently been halted. All this strengthened the resolve of those who stayed behind to wrest the ownership of the land from the alien landlord and to restore it to the people. The success of that resolve has had a considerable influence both on the country's subsequent development and on the present character of the Irish Republic.

Throughout the second half of the eighteenth century, though the majority of the population remained very poor, Irish agriculture was fairly prosperous – especially during the Napoleonic wars when a substantial market for Irish grain and dairy produce developed in Britain. After 1815 the wartime boom collapsed, the pattern of British demand for Irish agricultural products changed and this precarious prosperity was destroyed. It was impossible however to reshape Irish agriculture to take advantage of this change by reverting to pasture farming, the traditional basis of Irish agriculture. It was impossible because in the seventy years between 1770 and 1840 the Irish population had doubled. It is still not clear why this happened when it did – reduced mortality and more stable food supplies seem to have been the most important factors – but it led inevitably to greater and greater competition for land. Holdings were divided and redivided (often without any regard for the fertility of the land), rents went on rising, wages remained almost static, and as land got scarcer and the population more numerous, the condition of the poorest – the cottiers – grew more and more desperate. Increasingly they were forced to rely on the potato as their major source of food. Their condition was well described by Alexis de Tocqueville when he visited Ireland in 1835:

'All the houses in line to my right and my left were made of sun-dried mud and built with walls the height of a man. The roofs of these dwellings were made of thatch so old that the grass which covered it could be confused with the meadows on the neighbouring hills. In more than one place I saw that the flimsy timbers supporting these fragile roofs had yielded to the effects of time, giving the whole thing the effect of a mole-hill on which a passer-by has trod. The houses mostly had neither windows nor chimneys: the daylight came in and smoke came out by the door. If one could see into the houses, it was rare to notice more than bare walls, a ricketty stool and a small peat fire burning slowly and dimly between four flat stones.'

In such circumstances it was clearly impossible to carry out the wholesale clearance of population and the consolidation of holdings that would have been necessary if agriculture was to be restructured for grazing. Many prophesied that the time would soon come when the land would no longer support the people; by 1841, in fact, when the population officially reached eight million, this time *had* come. Conditions were worst in the south and west where population growth had been fastest and where holdings were smallest. Of the 820,000 or so holdings recorded in 1841, 330,000 were smaller than five acres, and 135,000 smaller than one acre. The families living on the smallest holdings were entirely dependent on the potato, but even on the smallest plot they could grow enough potatoes to feed a family of six. Without the potato two million people would have starved.

Every year, after one potato crop had been finished and before another could be lifted, many went hungry; and several times in the early nineteenth century there were serious local famines. When the potato crop was struck by blight in 1845, it seemed at first to be just another temporary difficulty. In 1846 however blight struck all over the country. Jonathan Pim recorded:

'The appearance of the potatoes was most favourable when suddenly they seemed blasted, as if by lightning. The leaves withered, the stalks became bare and black, the whole plant was dead, while the tubers were in many places scarcely formed, and in no part of the country were the late potatoes fully grown. The crop was destroyed. The food of a whole people was cut off.'

The winter that followed was one of the harshest of the century. Want and misery spread and disease rapidly followed – typhus and relapsing fever, scurvy and dysentery. 1847 was a year of considerable suffering, and though the potato crop was sound, few potatoes were planted because most of the seed potatoes had been eaten during the previous winter. In 1848 the potato crop failed again. Famine struck unevenly – starvation and disease were most severe in the south and west, less so in the north and east, but few parts of the country escaped altogether. The length, the scale, and the extent of the disaster were without parallel:

'Go where you might, every object reminded you of the fearful desolation that was progressing around you. The features of the people were gaunt, their eyes wild and hollow, and their gait feeble and tottering. Pass through the fields, and you were met by little groups bearing home on their shoulders, and that with difficulty, a coffin, or perhaps two of them. The roads were literally black with funerals, and as you passed along from parish to parish the death bells were pealing forth.'

At first many people, notably groups like the Quakers, but also many landlords, clergymen and doctors, did all they could to relieve the suffering. But even their gallant and unselfish efforts could make little impact; only the concerted action of government could have made any impression on the problem.

At first the British government did make a vigorous effort to provide alternative supplies of food. Sir Robert Peel, the prime minister, arranged for £100,000 worth of maize to be bought in America, shipped to Cork, and sold at specially low prices. At the same time over half a million pounds was given to local authorities in grants and loans to establish public works projects so that people would have money to buy food.

In June 1846 however Peel's government was defeated and replaced by a Whig administration under Lord John Russell. The Whigs were not prepared to spend government money on buying food, or on subsidising its sale, and they were not prepared to spend government money on public works. Charles Trevelyan, the Assistant Secretary to the Treasury, who was responsible for co-ordinating the relief of distress, wrote: 'There is only one way in which the relief of the destitute ever has been, or ever will be, conducted consistently with the general welfare, and that is by making it a local charge.'

What this meant in practice was that relief must be limited to the provision of public works paid out of a local rate levied on Irish landowners – Irish poverty must be supported by Irish property. Between September and December 1846 however the number of people dependent on relief shot up from 26,000 to 500,000. The system broke down and the government was forced to renew the distribution of free food through government soup kitchens. By the summer of 1847 three million people were receiving free daily rations. At the same time the government was forced to close down the public works and allow the destitute to be relieved in the workhouses.

The workhouses were already overcrowded in 1847, and by 1849 there were nearly a million inmates in a system designed to hold 100,000. But so many clamoured for admission that by 1849 another 800,000 were receiving assistance outside the workhouse. Because of an amendment to the Poor Law in 1847 (the so-called Gregory Clause) no one with more than $\frac{1}{4}$ acre of land could enter the workhouse unless they gave it up. Many died rather than give up their land, but the fact that so many clamoured for admission showed how desperate they were – and, once admitted, many more died inside the workhouses. The local boards of poor law guardians were made legally liable for the whole cost of this relief, but in the end – because of the amount of money involved – the government had to cancel the debt.

As rents fell and rates rose many landowners were ruined. But even if all of them *had* paid, it would still have been impossible to finance relief on the scale that was needed out of the poor rate. As it was, landlords were still responsible for the rates levied on holdings worth less than £4, even if the rent wasn't paid. Many responded by evicting their tenants; during 1849 and 1850 200,000 people were evicted. And so 'the system intended to relieve the poor, by making the landlords responsible for their welfare, has at once made it the interest of the landlords to get rid of them'.

In the crisis years of 1845-1849 at least a million people died in Ireland of hunger and disease. Many have since reacted, like Charles Gavan Duffy, with the cry that the famine was 'a fearful murder committed on the mass of the people', or like John Mitchel, who could see nothing in the famine policy of the government but 'machinery deliberately devised and skilfully worked for the entire subjugation of the island – the slaughter of a portion of its people and the pauperisation of the rest'.

Charles Trevelyan, in particular, has frequently been attacked for the apparent inhumanity of his attitude. In July 1846, for example, he wrote to Sir Randolph Routh in Dublin about the public works scheme financed by the previous government. 'The only way to prevent the people from becoming habitually dependent on Government is to bring the operation to a close.... Whatever may be done hereafter these things should be stopped *now*, or you run the risk of paralysing all private enterprise and having this country on you for an indefinite number of years.' But Trevelyan was only reflecting the accepted economic orthodoxy of the time – the laissez-faire ideas of the so-called Manchester school. Russell's government, whose agent Trevelyan was, genuinely believed that state aid would diminish people's self-reliance and prolong the crisis, that food must not be distributed free because it would encourage idleness and upset the normal channels of trade. It is perhaps not unreasonable to ask, as one modern historian does 'whether the English government would have been equally faithful to the Manchester school had famine broken out in, say, Manchester'. But, as he goes on to admit, nineteenth century governments tended to regard the sufferings of the poor as part of the natural order of things, and Irish sufferings were not unique, even in the 1840s; 72,000 people died of cholera in England and Wales between June and October 1848 – a significant proportion of them in Manchester. It's doubtful, finally, if *any* system of relief could have coped with disaster on this scale. The relief of widespread famine in Asia is difficult enough even today; it was considerably more difficult in the 1840s. When all this is said, however, it must be recognised that the famine has left an indelible mark on the popular memory: 'Between Ireland and England, the memory of what was done and endured has lain like a sword'.

It had beeen expected that the population of Ireland in 1851 would have been about nine million: in fact, it was $6\frac{1}{2}$ million, 2 million less than in 1845. A million had died. The other million had left the country in a headlong flight to get out of what seemed to them a doomed land. A fair number of people had emigrated in the 1820s and 1830s, but now this trickle became a flood; what had once been regarded as a last resort was now thought of as a welcome release. 'All we want', said one group, 'is to get out of Ireland. We must be better anywhere than here.'

During the famine and for several years after it an average of 200,000 people emigrated from Ireland every year. In the ten years between 1845 and 1855, 2 million people left the country. Many went to Britain, more to Canada and Australia and most to the United States. Not all the emigrants, especially in the early years, were those hardest hit by the famine. Many respectable farmers, wrote a contemporary: 'cut the corn on the Sunday, sell it on Monday morning, and are off to America in the evening, leaving the waste lands behind them and the landlords without rent'. Landlords too paid the passages of some emigrants, either from a genuine desire to help, or to clear their land of unwanted tenants. For those who were left behind, the moment of parting was like a death in the family:

'A deafening wail resounds as the station-bell gives the signal of starting. I have seen grey-haired peasants so clutch and cling to the departing child at this last moment that only the utmost force of three or four friends could tear them asunder. The porters have to use some violence before the train moves off, the crowd so presses against door and window. When at length it moves away, amidst a scene of passionate grief, hundreds run along the fields beside the line to catch yet another glimpse of the friends they shall see no more.'[1]

The passage to America was frequently appalling. The ships in which the emigrants sailed were mostly small cargo vessels, and even the best cargo ships were quite unsuitable for passengers – 'The friendless emigrants stowed away like bales of cotton and packed like slaves in a slave ship'. For forty days they spent the whole time below decks crowded in squalid, airless and insanitary quarters, battened under hatches in bad weather – 'We had not been at sea one week when to hold your head down the forehatch was like holding it down a suddenly opened cesspool'. In such conditions disease spread like wildfire; in 1847 40,000 of the 230,000 emigrants died at sea. A survivor recalled:

'The girl died, and from the middle of one day until six o'clock the next, before the captain would open the hatches, she and the dead girl were there; and when the vessel would lurch, it seemed to her that the corpse would open its eyes and mouth.'

Though emigration from Ireland was most dramatic in the years after the famine, people continued to leave Ireland whenever times were bad, especially during the depression of 1877-1882. By 1900 there were as many Irishmen *outside* the British Isles as there were inside, and three quarters of those outside Ireland were in the United States. Between 1851 and 1900 three million Irish men and women emigrated to America – a human chain created by the succession of remittances sent back to pay the passages of those who had stayed behind, and constantly encouraged by the vision of the New World described in the thousands of emigrants' letters that accompanied them:

'My dear Father, I must only say that this is a good place and a good country'; 'Come to this country and I know you will do well'; 'I still think I am in as good a country as there is in the world today for a poor man'; 'If some of our hardy men of Tipperary were here, what a fortune would be open to them'; 'America is a country for every man of energy and industry to rise to respectability and independence.'

Many emigrants carried with them to America a burning hatred of England and a desire for revenge. Once they had become established most of them contented themselves with applauding rabble-rousing speeches and with liberal donations to Irish causes, though they were a group whose views any British government had increasingly to take into account. For a few, however, America was the base from which they would finance and plan an Irish rebellion which would defeat the English and establish an Irish Republic – the lever, as John Mitchel said, that would turn the world.

As emigration continued, especially to the United States, so the population of Ireland continued to fall – indeed it's only just stopped. Today the population of

EMIGRATION 1851-1971
(32 counties 1851-1911, 26 counties 1926-71)
(figures rounded to nearest thousand)

	Population	Emigration
1841	8,175,000	
1851	6,552,000	
1852-60		1,011,000
1861	5,799,000	
1861-70		850,000
1871	5,412,000	
1871-80		624,000
1881	5,175,000	
1881-90		771,000
1891	4,705,000	
1891-1900		434,000
1901	4,459,000	
1901-1910		346,000
1911	4,390,000	
1911-1926		405,000*
1926	2,972,000	
1926-36		167,000
1936	2,968,000	
1936-46		187,000
1946	2,955,000	
1946-51		120,000
1951	2,961,000	
1951-56		197,000
1956	2,898,000	
1956-61		212,000
1961	2,818,000	
1961-66		81,000
1966	2,884,000	
1966-71		54,000
1971	2,978,000	

*from 1911-26 onwards figures are for estimated *net* emigration

the whole island, Northern Ireland and the Republic, is about 4½ million, little over half what it was in 1841 just before the famine.

This fall has been concentrated in the countryside. Between 1841 and 1911 the rural population declined from 5½ million to 2¼ million. Most of those who left the countryside moreover were those who, before the famine, had occupied the smallest plots of land. Holdings of between 1 and 5 acres for example fell from 182,000 just before the famine to 62,000 in 1911, and holdings of between 5 and 15 acres from 311,000 to 154,000; but holdings of between 15 and 30 acres actually rose a little.

Before the famine – though this had begun to change in the 1830s – Ireland had been a country of early marriages; afterwards fewer and later marriages became the pattern. The most likely reasons for this seem to be a combination of Catholic teaching about chastity and the deep reluctance of the Irish farmer ever again to contemplate the fragmentation of his holding. Whatever the reason, the result was that, by the end of the nineteenth century, the 15-30 acre family farm had begun to emerge as the typical unit of Irish agriculture.

The farm was handed down to the farmer's eldest son. Since he usually could not afford to get married until he owned the farm, he sometimes never got married at all. The other children emigrated. What had once been a rural proletariat began to develop rapidly into a rural bourgeoisie. Indeed the number of farm labourers in Ireland, the only remaining members of this proletariat, declined from more than 1·3 million before the famine to fewer than 250,000 in 1911. There was some tension between these landless men and the more substantial tenant farmers which occasionally exploded into violence, and which provided a fertile recruiting ground for extremist organisations from the Fenians in the 1860s to the IRA in the 1920s. Emigration however prevented this tension from ever becoming a serious threat.

Finally, the famine was a fatal blow for many landlords. As a result of the Encumbered Estates Act of 1849 (which was passed to make the sale and transfer of the estates of ruined landlords easier) some 5 million acres – about a quarter of all the land in the country – changed hands in the thirty years after the famine. Many of the new landlords were Catholics, some of them hard-faced men who had done well out of the famine:

'Of all the landowning classes at that period' wrote Henry Robinson some years later, 'none were more hated and feared than the ex-gombeen men [money lenders] who had invested their ill-gotten gains in the purchase of small insolvent estates coming up for sale in the Landed Estates Courts.'

Popular mythology exaggerated both their numbers and their vices; more often than not this hostility seems to have been caused by a combination of distaste for their humble origin and envy of their success. It seems fairly clear however that many of the new landlords were less paternalistic than the old and more concerned with the efficient use of the land. A few years later an authority on land tenures wrote that: 'The new landlords were more active and effected more improvements in the land than their encumbered predecessors, but they were less indulgent to their tenants; old traditions of liberality were disregarded and the new landlords were disposed to exact the full value of the land.'

They were especially keen to take advantage of the growing and profitable market in England for Irish livestock which had opened up with the development of the railways. The amount of land under tillage nearly halved in the fifty years after the famine, to just under $2\frac{1}{2}$ million acres – and the acreage under grain by two-thirds – but meadow and pasture rose by nearly a quarter, to 13 million acres. At the same time the number of cattle doubled, and cattle exports rose four times to a peak of 835,000 a year.

The twenty years after the famine were good times on the land. Rents – which were in any case based on a very low valuation – remained remarkably stable, but stock prices more than doubled, and this led to a dramatic rise in farmers' incomes. Bank deposits in Ireland doubled between 1845 and 1859[2], and doubled again between 1859 and 1876, and the consumption of both tea and tobacco rose almost to English levels by the 1870s.

Prosperity was not however universal. In the far west, especially in the coastal areas of Donegal, Mayo, Galway and Kerry, the population actually continued to increase after the famine. A growing population bidding for land, small farms being subdivided into even smaller farms, and dependence on the potato, perpetuated exactly that combination of circumstances that had made the famine so terrible. When, for three successive years in the late 1870s, the potato crop failed, distress in the west was again widespread and severe. In the 1870s however the resources for dealing with it were both far better developed and far more effectively applied. But what turned this local disaster into a national crisis was that it coincided with a severe agricultural depression. Foreign competition, falling prices and bad harvests threatened the new-found prosperity of thousands of farmers.

Ever since the famine, there had been steady pressure from tenants – especially during the Tenant Right movement of the 1850s – for greater security in their holdings.[3] This pressure was recognised by Gladstone, who passed a Land Act in 1870 which attempted, unsuccessfully, to give tenants this increased security. Though it largely failed in its objectives, however, by recognising that tenants had an interest in their holdings, it established an entirely new legal principle and undermined the traditional landlord/tenant relationship.

When the bottom fell out of the market for agricultural products in 1877 and 1878, more and more tenant farmers became unable to pay their rents and all were liable to be evicted. In the three years between 1878 and

[2] Some of this may have been due to the great increase in the number of the banks' branches between 1845 and 1870; some of the apparent increase in savings may therefore simply represent transfers from under the mattress.

[3] The political significance of the Tenant Right movement is discussed in chapter 3 (pp. 32–42).

1880 the number of evictions increased sharply. It was not surprising therefore that Michael Davitt, appalled by conditions in his native Mayo, should have had an immediate success with the Land League.

The League was established in October 1879, at first to relieve distress, but increasingly it became concerned to prevent evictions, reduce rents, and eventually to secure the ownership of the land for the people. Davitt claimed that 'Land being created to supply mankind with the necessaries of existence, those who cultivate it to that end have a higher claim to its absolute possession than those who make it an article of barter to be used or disposed of for purposes of profit or pleasure'. He was drawing on an older tradition, a tradition eloquently expressed 30 years earlier by James Fintan Lalor at the height of the famine:
'The soil of Ireland for the people of Ireland, to have and to hold from God alone who gave it – to have and to hold to them and their heirs for ever.'

The Land League's main weapon in their fight was a rent strike. The withholding of rent led to more evictions. The Land League arranged for evictions to be accompanied by popular demonstrations, for the defence of tenants prosecuted in the courts and for the shelter and support of their families. It was also prepared to enforce solidarity by threatening reprisals on those who broke ranks – especially on 'grabbers' who occupied land which had been taken from evicted tenants. All this was inevitably accompanied by violence – the burning of ricks, the maiming of cattle, the shooting of landlords and their agents – and sometimes also of grabbers and their families. Violence of peasant towards peasant in fact was probably worse than that of peasant towards landlord.

But the Land League's success was due not to violence but to the generous subscriptions of the American Irish – who were contributing £1,000 a week to the League's funds by the end of 1880 – and to general support for the League's policy of organised social ostracism. This policy was outlined in a famous speech by Charles Stewart Parnell at Ennis in September 1880.[4] 'When a man takes a farm from which another has been unjustly evicted, you must shun him on the roadside when you meet him; you must shun him in the streets of the town; you must shun him in the shop; you must shun him in the fair green and in the market place; and even in the place of worship, by leaving him alone; by putting him into a moral coventry; by isolating him from the rest of his country as if he were the leper of old.'

One of the earliest – and certainly the most famous – victim of this policy was Lord Erne's Agent, Captain Boycott.

It became increasingly difficult for landlords to evict, and even if this was successful, it was just as difficult to re-let the land; rents dwindled away to the point at which many landlords were threatened with ruin. There was considerable feeling in England that the system was unjust and that the landlords were somehow to blame for all the trouble, but there was equal concern that the fundamental rights of property should not be threatened, especially by violence. Somehow the majority of moderates had to be pacified and split off from the minority of extremists. When, in 1881, a Royal Commission recommended a further and more radical measure of land reform, Gladstone accepted it and introduced a Land Act designed, in his words, for 'the relief of Ireland's ancient wrongs'. The 1881 Act was designed to establish fair rents, fixity of tenure and a free market in land (known as the three 'F's). In fact it was essentially a rent control act. Land Courts were established to fix a 'judicial rent'; what this meant in practice was that rents were reduced to the level which tenants would accept. The result was that in the ten years following the Act, rents fell by up to 25 per cent, and when they were reviewed again, in 1896, many fell even further – by up to 40 per cent. At this level, many landlords – whose fixed costs remained the same – simply ceased to make any money from their land and some lost heavily.

But the 1881 Act also established an important new principle. The 1870 Act had recognised the tenants' claim to some interest in his land; now the tenant was

[4] Parnell's career is examined in greater detail in chapter 3 (pp. 39–42).

Page 30 and 31: four contemporary photographs of evictions during the land war. The before and after pair on page 30 illustrate not only the effectiveness of the battering ram, but also the involvement of both soldiers and police on such occasions. On page 31 neighbours are seen saying the rosary before an eviction (top) and an evicted family is seen (bottom) outside the boarded-up door of their cabin, their few possessions scattered on the ground beside them.

regarded as an equal partner with his landlord – or, as a contemporary put it, landlord and tenant had been placed in the same bed, and the tenant now attempted – with remarkable success – to kick the landlord out.

In fact the landlords' situation was extremely unsatisfactory. Owning land was now neither profitable nor pleasant and landlords became increasingly willing to dispose of the burden to their tenants. But although both the 1870 and 1881 Land Acts had contained provisions for tenants to buy their land, the proposals were not attractive enough either to the tenant or to the landlord. 'If the government and Parliament mean business in this matter', resolved the Landowners Convention, 'they must deal with it in a businesslike manner by a more liberal use of the great asset at their disposal – the credit of the British Exchequer.' What this meant was that the British Exchequer would have to bridge the gap between the price the owners could afford to take and the price the tenants could afford to give.

Gradually the British government came to accept this proposal in full. Between 1885 and 1903 60,000 tenant farmers bought their land, and after the Wyndham Act of 1903, 250,000 more did so. By 1908 nearly half the farmers in Ireland owned their own land and by 1917 two thirds did so. Finally, in 1923, the government of the Irish Free State made the sale of the few remaining estates compulsory and the power of the landlord was extinguished. 'The League', wrote Davitt, 'found the Irish peasant a virtual slave on the land of Ireland. It has "rooted" him in the soil on which he was but a rent-earning machine and has given him a right of property, where he was previously but a trespasser, equal to that of his former master.'

And so a social revolution – begun by the famine and accelerated by the Land League – had been achieved. But this social revolution was not accompanied, as it was in many other European countries, by an economic revolution. By concentrating her energies on the struggle to secure the land for the people, Ireland failed to adapt and modernise her agriculture. The result has been that the peasant proprietor – men like poor Paddy Maguire in P. J. Kavanagh's poem *The Great Hunger* – who was once the hero of a national struggle, has become one of the Irish Republic's most pressing problems:

Who bent the coin of my destiny
That it stuck in the slot?
I remember a night we walked
Through the moon of Donaghmoyne
Four of us seeking adventure
It was midsummer forty years ago.
Now I know
The moment that gave the turn to my life
O Christ! I am locked in a stable with pigs and cows for ever

GOD SAVE IRELAND

The rebellion of 1798 established a tradition of revolutionary violence which has never died out of Irish politics. In 1848, in 1867, and finally in the Easter Rising in 1916, the Irish turned again to rebellion to break the connection with England. Each successive rebellion looked back to the one before, and all to the example of 1798. And the Irishman whose ideas had the greatest influence on the later risings was Wolfe Tone, one of the founders of the Society of United Irishmen in 1791. It was Wolfe Tone whom Patrick Pearse, the moving spirit of the Easter Rising, recalled in June 1913, when he said:

'My brothers, were it not an unspeakable privilege if to our generation it should be granted to accomplish that which Tone's generation, so much worthier than ours, failed to accomplish.'

In December 1921 Pearse's generation accomplished the separation of 26 of the 32 Irish counties from Britain and the establishment of the Irish Free State.

But for most of the period between the rebellion of 1798 and the establishment of the Free State, it had seemed that if separation *were* to take place, it would take place as the result of constitutional agitation. Catholic Emancipation was achieved in 1829, not by violence, but as the result of a campaign by the first organised mass movement in British politics. O'Connell's Repeal campaign in the 1840s was run on strictly constitutional lines. Parnell's Home Rule movement in the 1880s was based on the Irish Nationalist parliamentary party; but though it drew much of its strength from the revolutionary potential of a mass movement rooted in the Irish countryside, Parnell was determined not to surrender to violence. And when, finally, a Home Rule Bill was passed by the British Parliament in 1914, it was greeted by Irish Nationalist MPs cheering and singing *God save the King*.

The rebellion of 1798, which had convinced both the British government and many Irish Protestants that their position could only be secured by Union with Britain, had also led many middle-class Catholics to the conclusion that their best chance of achieving complete equality with Protestants was to support the Union as well. William Pitt, the British Prime Minister, had originally intended that Union should be accompanied by Catholic Emancipation, and middle class Catholics had supported Union on the understanding that this would happen. But opposition, especially from George III, forced Pitt to abandon Emancipation as a condition of the Union, and when this opposition continued to prevent Emancipation, Pitt resigned. If Emancipation had been built into the Act of Union in 1800 there would have been a real incentive for Catholics and Protestants to work together and Catholics would have had a vested interest in the new system. As it was, the Irish administration in Dublin Castle remained in the hands of the same people who had always controlled it – the Protestant Ascendancy.

For the next few years there were regular attempts – all of them ineffective – to raise the question of Emancipation at Westminster. They were led by the Protestant Henry Grattan and got little support from Catholics. In May 1823 however Daniel O'Connell founded the Catholic Association to win equal rights for Catholics.

O'Connell was a Catholic, the son of a small Co. Kerry landowner, who had made a brilliant career at the Bar. But although both his background and his experience made him a conservative, he had some radical ideas, and he was a great public speaker with a genius for public relations. In February 1824, O'Connell changed the rules of the Catholic Association so that people could become members for a subscription of one penny a month instead of the guinea a year that had previously been necessary. More important than the size of the 'Catholic Rent' that this produced – £60,000 in six years – the expansion of its membership transformed the Catholic Association from a small and genteel middle-class organisation into a national mass-movement. But though this popular movement was potentially a revolutionary weapon, O'Connell used it for constitutional agitation which had strictly limited aims.

Most of the voters in the Irish county constituencies were Catholics, and under O'Connell's influence they now began to use their votes in favour of Emancipation.

In defiance of their landlords, and with the whole-hearted support of the Catholic clergy, these voters returned a handful of Emancipation candidates in the 1826 Election. In 1828 O'Connell himself stood at a by-election in Co. Clare. Although, as a Catholic, he couldn't take his seat if he won, O'Connell won a resounding victory. The defeated candidate, William Vesey Fitzgerald declared: 'The organisation exhibited is so complete and so formidable that no man can contemplate without alarm what is to follow in this country'. But rather than face the equally unpalatable alternatives of coercion, or an un-ending series of by-elections, Wellington's ultra-conservative administration gave in. What followed, in April 1829, was virtually complete Catholic Emancipation – the removal of practically all the remaining formal restrictions on Catholics. At the same time, however, the Catholic Association was disbanded and the Irish county franchise qualifications raised from 40 shillings to £10.

Emancipation was significant for both sides. For Catholics it suggested that concessions could only be wrung out of a reluctant Britain by a mass demonstration of Catholic solidarity. For Protestants it appeared to confirm a growing conviction that, to Catholics, only Catholics were really Irishmen, and that their own security depended on union with Britain. For as O'Connell wrote to a friend: 'How mistaken men are who suppose that the history of the world will be over as soon as we are emancipated! Oh, *that* will be the time to *commence* the struggle for popular rights'.

In fact, however, though O'Connell began to mount his next campaign – for the Repeal of the Act of Union – almost at once, the triumph of 1829 was followed by a long anti-climax, which lasted until 1840. O'Connell became the leader of a small group of Repeal MPs in the House of Commons, but when he introduced a motion for Repeal in 1834 it was defeated by 529 votes to 38 (all from his own party). For whereas there had been widespread support, both in Parliament and in the country at large, for Catholic Emancipation, there was equally widespread opposition to Repeal. As a result, O'Connel[l] ... [p]olicy of 'Testing the Union', suppo[rting] ... [g]overnment in return for reforms, and [between] ... and 1840 a number of useful reforms were [secured] in this way. As O'Connell said: 'I will get wh[at] I can, and use the Repeal *in terrorem* merely, until it is wise and necessary to recommence the agitation'. But the results of O'Connell's opportunist policy, though considerable, were not as favourable as he had hoped. His popularity in Ireland suffered, and the 'O'Connell Tribute' which had succeeded the 'Catholic Rent' began to dwindle alarmingly. When a Whig government was replaced by the Tories in 1841, O'Connell turned back again to Repeal.

He had already founded the Loyal National Repeal Association in 1840. At first it had little success, but this soon changed – firstly, because of the renewed support of the Catholic clergy, and secondly because of the influence of the *Nation*. This newspaper was founded by Thomas Davis, John Blake Dillon and Charles Gavan Duffy in October 1842, and represented the views of a group of young men who became known as Young Ireland. The Repeal Association was based, as the Catholic Association had been based, on O'Connell's personality, good organisation, the support of the Catholic clergy, effective propaganda and a Repeal Rent – which was soon raising £2,000 a week. O'Connell declared that 1843 would be Repeal Year. The main weapon in the campaign was to be a series of monster meetings. At one of the forty meetings Lord Lytton described the audience as 'a human ocean' which 'wave on wave flowed into space away'; and contemporaries claimed that a million people assembled to hear O'Connell speak on the hill of Tara in August 1843.

He stood erect, took off his cap, the countless crowd to hail,
With three cheers for Queen Victoria and nine thousand for
*   Repeal.*
The dusky clouds of Heaven cleared, bright Sol diffused his
*   beams,*
The foggy mist expelled far raised off the mountains stream –
When Dan approached the papal spot all nature seemed to
*   smile.*
This day shall never be forgot throughout Hibernia's Isle.

O'Connell's aim was to overawe the government by the size and discipline of the occasions. 'I want you to do nothing that is not open and loyal, but if the people unite with me and follow my advice it is impossible not to get the Repeal', he said at one meeting, and at another: 'When such a combination is complete, the Parliament will naturally yield to the wishes and prayer of an entire nation. It is not in the nature of things that it should be otherwise'. The British government, however, far from being overawed by such demonstrations, was determined to reassert its authority. 'I feel and know that the Repeal must lead to the dismemberment of this great Empire' said the Prime Minister, Sir Robert Peel. 'There is no influence, no power, no authority, which the prerogatives of the Crown and the existing law gives to the Government which will not be exercised for the purpose of maintaining the Union.'

In October 1843 the government banned a monster meeting at Clontarf a few hours before it was due to take place and O'Connell at once called it off. This might have been a serious blow, both to O'Connell's prestige and to the Repeal campaign, if the government had not then charged O'Connell and his colleagues with conspiracy. They were found guilty and imprisoned (though they managed to make themselves remarkably comfortable). They appealed to the House of Lords and the verdict was quashed.

After his release, in September 1844, O'Connell resumed his campaign. In 1845 there was another series of monster meetings and the Repeal Rent rose to new heights. Developments in England encouraged O'Connell to believe that political pressure would, sooner or later, pay off, and he began for the first time to make a serious attempt to influence public opinion in England in favour of Repeal.

But some of the younger, more radical and less sophisticated amongst his supporters – especially in the Young Ireland group who ran the *Nation* – began to become dissatisfied with O'Connell's leadership. O'Connell was an aristocrat and a constitutionalist. The first principle of the Repeal Association was: 'Most dutiful and ever inviolate loyalty to our most gracious and ever beloved Sovereign Queen Victoria and her heirs and successors for ever.'
Secondly, whatever he might say to the contrary, O'Connell was a loyal son of the Church whose close connections with the Roman Catholic clergy alienated and alarmed Irish Protestants. As he once said of them in the House of Commons: 'They are foreigners to us since they are of a different religion'.

Young Ireland, on the other hand, which – like the United Irishmen – was very much an urban middle-class organisation with many Protestant members, was also – like the United Irishmen – genuinely ecumenical. 'Cease to live in hostile camps at home as Protestants and Catholics' wrote Thomas Davis. 'Your interests as Irishmen are absolutely identical.' They had an equally strong belief in Ireland's national identity – as Davis said: 'This country of ours is no sandbank, thrown up by some recent caprice of earth. It is an ancient land, honoured in the archives of civilisation, traceable into antiquity by its piety, its valour and its sufferings'.

Overleaf: a remarkable example of the persistence of a stereotype. On page 36, a cartoon by Meadows from Punch, *4 November 1843, and on page 37 another by Tenniel from* Punch, *20 May 1882. The Simian Irishman was to reappear in* Punch *as late as 1920.*

The breach came in 1845 over Peel's plan for non-denominational university colleges in Cork, Galway and Belfast. Young Ireland supported Peel, O'Connell opposed these 'godless colleges' on the grounds that Catholic morals could only be safeguarded by segregated education. The next year O'Connell manoeuvred Young Ireland out of the Repeal Association by insisting on 'the total disclaimer of, and the total absence from, all physical force, violence or breach of the law'.

Soon afterwards O'Connell died, but by then the famine had begun to change the whole context of the debate. It led James Fintan Lalor, one of Young Ireland's most eloquent spokesmen, to declare that society stood dissolved, that 'the entire ownership of Ireland, moral and material, up to the sun, and down to the centre, is vested of right in the people of Ireland' and that 'this full right of ownership may and ought to be asserted and enforced by any and all means which God has put into the power of man'.

The Repeal campaign was submerged by the famine, but some Young Irelanders had already reached the conclusion that constitutional methods were ineffective and that national independence could only be achieved by force. In 1848 a great wave of revolution swept over Europe – in Germany, in Italy, and especially in France where the monarchy was overthrown and a republic established. Even in England there were massive demonstrations by the Chartists demanding votes for all. All this convinced even the most moderate Young Irelanders that this was indeed the Year of Revolution. Ignoring the fact that Ireland in the grip of famine was in no condition for a successful rebellion, Young Ireland prepared for a rising. They lacked the arms, the numbers, the leadership, even the determination necessary for success. The revolution ended in August 1848 with a brief skirmish in a back garden in Co. Tipperary; the leaders were captured and transported.

Though in practical terms it achieved nothing, the rising of 1848 quickly took its place in the revolutionary canon which stretches from 1798 to Easter 1916. It kept alive the idea that Ireland was a separate nation and that the historic rights of that nation might justify violence to achieve her independence. But to many Englishmen, tired of being made to feel guilty about the famine, it seemed to confirm that the Irish were ungrateful, irresponsible and treacherous and unfit to govern themselves.

'Repeal was buried' wrote a contemporary observer. 'Disaffection had disappeared. Nationality was unmentioned. Not a shout was raised. The people no longer interested themselves in politics. All was silence.'

Not quite all. It was obviously easier to pick up the threads of a constitutional than of a revolutionary organisation. During the 1850s another attempt was made to create an independent parliamentary party at Westminster, and through this to work for the solution of the land problem by what was called 'tenant right': the right of tenants to profit from improvements made to their holdings when they sold them. At first the movement was strong in both north and south, but Protestants in the north became less active when they saw how closely the Catholic clergy were involved. In any case the party lacked the leadership, the organisation and the resources of the Repeal movement. When two of its leading members accepted office in the Aberdeen government in 1853, and when leading members of the Catholic hierarchy opposed the movement as an attack on private property, it soon disintegrated. 48 Independent MPs were elected in 1852; by 1859 there were none. The fact that prosperity returned so quickly to the countryside in the 1850s also helped to make the question of tenant right seem less important to the voters.

The main consequence was to increase popular contempt both for parliamentary parties and constitutional methods and to establish a favourable climate for a swing back to militancy. James Stephens, who had been 'out' in 1848 and had afterwards escaped to Paris, returned to Ireland in 1856 and walked 3,000 miles round the countryside to test the mood of the people. As a result, in 1858 he founded a new society 'to make

THE IRISH FRANKENSTEIN.

THE IRISH FRANKENSTEIN.

Ireland an independent democratic republic' – if necessary by force, for 'I don't believe the Saxon will ever relax his grip except by the persuasion of cold lead and steel'. At first referred to as 'the organisation', 'the society', or 'the brotherhood', it later became, officially, the Irish Republican Brotherhood, and, unofficially, the Fenians.

The Fenians were a secret, oath-bound, underground organisation, and the reintroduction of the conspiratorial element into Irish nationalism was the movement's major significance. The Fenians grew rapidly, and though its own estimate of 80,000 members was certainly exaggerated, the movement did have a considerable following all over Ireland. It had also had a large membership in the United States, where the Brotherhood was organised by John O'Mahony, another refugee from 1848, who had been in Paris with Stephens. This division of the movement between Ireland and the USA was a fruitful source of disagreement – especially since America was the main source of funds. This was exacerbated by Stephens, who had a grotesquely inflated sense of his own importance and behaved accordingly.

Though some priests were sympathetic, the movement had a strong anti-clerical flavour, and the church's official attitude was succinctly put by Archbishop Cullen; it was, he said, 'a compound of folly and wickedness'. The Catholic church's opposition was a considerable disadvantage to the Fenians. Partly to counteract the church's influence, and partly to spread their own, Stephens resorted to the expedient – unusual, to say the least, for a secret society – of establishing a newspaper. *The Irish People*, founded in 1863, was a paper of unusual quality, but undoubtedly helped to make the movement vulnerable to informers. In 1865, when Stephens declared a year of action, the government was able to arrest the leaders immediately. Rivalries within the movement caused further delays, and when in 1867 a rising finally did take place, the government knew all about it in advance. Though to begin with the Fenians had several local successes, they lacked the arms, the money and the organisation

to sustain them and the rising was quickly suppressed. But while it lasted it caused considerable alarm in Britain.

This alarm was increased when later in the year the violence spread to Britain too. In September 1867 a policeman was killed in an attempt to rescue Fenians from a prison van in Manchester, and in December 12 people were killed and 30 injured in an attempt to dynamite the walls of Clerkenwell gaol. Three men were hanged – on suspect evidence – for the shooting of the Manchester policeman. This verdict was received with satisfaction in England, where the events of 1867 served only to increase the contempt which many felt for the Irish. In Ireland on the other hand the sentences created considerable popular sympathy for the 'Manchester Martyrs' and their cause. One of the condemned men, Edward Condon, had said from the dock 'I have nothing to regret, to retract or take back. I can only say 'God Save Ireland'. Overnight 'God Save Ireland' became the chorus of a song which was soon the unofficial national anthem. Once again the revolutionary myth became more important than what had actually happened, and 1867 joined 1848 and 1798 in the revolutionary canon. And the Fenians remained in being, especially in the United States.

And there was another, equally significant consequence. The events of 1867 conditioned many people in Britain 'to embrace, in a manner foreign to their habits at other times, the vast importance of the Irish controversy'. The words were Gladstone's, and he had become convinced that something would have to be done. 'My mission' he said, when he was asked to form his first government in 1868 'is to pacify Ireland'. He certainly made a serious attempt to do so, first by disestablishing the Church of Ireland in 1869, and so destroying the power of the established church and a traditional source of Catholic discontent;[1] and then in 1870 by passing the first Land Act to recognise that tenants had rights as well as landlords.

Throughout the 1860s a small group of Irish MPs

[1] See chapter 10 (pp. 122–129).

had continued – with a restraint that almost bordered on invisibility – to champion the idea that Ireland was a separate nation with a right to her own parliament. In 1870, encouraged by Gladstone's new policy, Isaac Butt formed the Home Government Association, dedicated to establishing such a parliament by constitutional methods – to achieving Home Rule for Ireland. Though their support for the Liberals failed to produce any more worthwhile reforms, in the 1874 election 59 Irish MPs were returned as Home Rulers. The Home Rulers however were not a coherent political party, but an uneasy and ill-disciplined coalition of conflicting interests. In 1875, after a by-election in Co. Meath, they were joined by a new member, Charles Stewart Parnell.

Parnell seemed an unlikely man to become a popular hero – a Protestant, a landlord, a country gentleman, educated in England. But one of his ancestors had opposed the Act of Union, and another had supported Catholic Emancipation. As a young man his imagination had been caught by the Fenians. And he hated the English: 'These Englishmen despise us because we are Irish, but we must stand up to them. That's the only way to treat an Englishman – stand up to him'.

It was natural therefore that he should ally himself in Parliament with a small group of Irish MPs who developed a campaign of obstructing the business of the House of Commons in an attempt to force English MPs to take their country's hopes seriously. Parnell's first notable remark in Parliament was that the men who had killed the policeman in the Fenian rescue attempt at Manchester ten years earlier had 'done no murder'. In 1877, in another speech, he said: 'We will never gain anything from England unless we tread upon her toes; we will never gain a single sixpennyworth from her by conciliation'. Such militancy attracted the attention of the Fenians. After only two years as an MP – largely with their support – Parnell became leader of the Home Rule organisation in England.

Meanwhile, a revolutionary situation was developing in the Irish countryside. The agricultural depression of the late 1870s had led to widespread distress, especially in the west, and to widespread evictions. In 1878 John Devoy (who was the effective leader of Clan na Gael, the American wing of the Fenians) decided – at least for the time being – to support the constitutional movement, if that movement was prepared to campaign against the landlords. This was indeed, as Devoy called it, a 'New Departure'.

Michael Davitt, the former Fenian who had founded the Land League, had been in close touch with Devoy over the New Departure; he now tried to persuade Parnell to join the campaign. In June 1879 Davitt and Devoy met Parnell in Dublin when they agreed, in Davitt's words, 'to an open participation in public movements by extreme men . . . in friendly rivalry with moderate nationalists'. Later the same month, Parnell went to Westport and gave the first of the speeches which rapidly brought him to the leadership of a truly national movement: 'You must show the landlords that you intend to keep a firm grip on your homesteads and lands. You must not allow yourselves to be dispossessed as you were dispossessed in 1847 . . . you must help yourselves and the public opinion of the world will stand by you and support you in your struggle to defend your homesteads'.

Parnell had grasped the key to a successful constitutional movement. It must be backed by a vigorous popular agitation in Ireland – with the threat of violence in the background – and the same man should control both the parliamentary party and the national agitation. Parnell intended to be that man. As Davitt said: 'The Fenians did not wish public attention to be fixed on Parliament. But Parnell fixed it on Parliament by fixing it on himself'. And again: 'He did not try to weaken the force of Fenianism, but he diverted it into a channel of his own choosing . . . He was always the master of himself, and ultimately became the master of us'.

In the autumn of 1879 Parnell became president of the Irish National Land League. In the general election of 1880, he had a personal triumph at the polls and became chairman of the Irish parliamentary party. For the next two years, Parnell balanced ambiguously between his role as the leader of the parliamentary party and his role as the leader of a mass movement trembling all the time on the verge of social revolution.

Gladstone had been returned to power once more in 1880. His Liberal government was sympathetic to Irish problems and had promised to introduce a Land Act which would guarantee tenants fair rents and security of tenure. But it was equally hostile to the violence in the Irish countryside and introduced a Coercion Bill to give the government special powers to deal with the situation. Parnell and his supporters reacted furiously – so furiously that he and 35 other Irish members were suspended and ejected from the House.

This was a crucial moment in Parnell's career. Some of his followers wanted the party to withdraw altogether from Parliament and work only through extremist agitation in Ireland. But Parnell knew that the Land Act would be popular among his moderate supporters and he was convinced that there were greater rewards to be reaped from parliamentary pressure. 'I would never have taken off my coat for the land question' he said, 'were it not a step on the road to Home Rule'.

At the same time Parnell had to keep in contact with the extremists and prevent the movement sliding into indiscriminate violence. His plan therefore was to see that the Land Act passed, and to continue to attack the government in fiery speeches which were mainly designed to impress his more extreme followers. The difficulty was that his speeches were apt to impress the government as much as they did his followers. In October 1881 Parnell and the other leaders of the Land League were arrested and imprisoned in Kilmainham prison in Dublin. When he was arrested Parnell said that 'Captain Moonlight' would take his place. And certainly, with the leaders of the Land League in prison, the 'wild men' took over and violence in the countryside increased once more.

Gladstone wanted to restore law and order, but he needed Parnell's authority to do it; Parnell needed to be free to re-assert his own leadership. The result was the so-called Kilmainham Treaty. Gladstone would end Coercion and extend the benefits of the Land Act. Parnell in return would use his influence against violence and intimidation in Ireland, and 'co-operate cordially for the future with the Liberal party in forwarding Liberal principles and measures of general reform'.

In May 1882 Parnell was released. Almost at once the Treaty was jeopardised by the assassination – by members of a secret society, the Invincibles – of the Chief Secretary for Ireland and his Under Secretary as they were walking in Phoenix Park, Dublin. But though the murders stirred up considerable public feeling in England, the agreement between Parnell and Gladstone survived. Indeed the success of the Land Act and the failure of violence had cut the ground from under the feet of the extremists. As Parnell had predicted in Kilmainham: 'Politically, it is a fortunate thing for me that I have been arrested, as the movement is breaking fast and all will be quiet in a few months when I shall be released'.

The revolutionary movement did indeed collapse and more and more moderates – especially in the Catholic church – rallied behind Parnell. At the end of 1882 Parnell launched the Irish National League, under the control of the parliamentary party, to organise and finance a national campaign for Home Rule. In the 1885 Election–with the number of voters trebled by franchise reform–this paid off handsomely, and Parnell returned to Westminster with a disciplined bloc of 86 Irish Nationalist MPs pledged to sit, act and vote together. By an extraordinary coincidence this was exactly the same as the Liberals' majority over the Conservatives. As the leader of an effective third party in the House of Commons Parnell no longer needed a mass movement; as the leader of a party which held the balance of power his position was even stronger.

Soon afterwards, Gladstone indicated that he was prepared to consider Home Rule. He was not however motivated primarily by the balance of power in the House of Commons. Gladstone had been increasingly impressed by the strength and persistence of Irish demands, the discipline and effectiveness of the Irish party and above all by Parnell's ability as their leader. He had for many years been concerned to secure a permanent solution to the Irish question which would take it out of British politics for good. For Gladstone, enlightened self-government was the highest stage of man's political evolution and he believed that the Irish were now ready for it. Accordingly, in 1886, he introduced a Home Rule Bill – Ireland was to have a parliament of her own, and limited control of her own affairs. But Gladstone could not carry his party with him. 93 Liberals voted with the Conservatives and the bill was defeated on its second reading by 30 votes. Gladstone resigned. To the MPs who opposed Home Rule it was a threat to the integrity and security of the British Empire; any weakness of the Imperial structure, they believed, would lead – sooner or later – to its complete disintegration. Many of them still thought of the Irish as backward and illiterate peasants, unfit to govern themselves. Many more did not trust Parnell. They could not be sure that; for Parnell, Home Rule was to be the final settlement. In one of his election speeches, after all, he had said: 'No man has the right to set a boundary to the onward march of a nation. No man has a right to say "Thus far and no further".'

But the defeat of the Home Rule Bill also meant that Parnell's freedom of manoeuvre had been drastically curtailed. If Home Rule could now only be obtained with Liberal support, then the Nationalists were at least as much at the Liberals' mercy as the Liberals were at theirs. Most important of all, by accepting that Home Rule could best be achieved if the Nationalists behaved as if they were just another political party, Parnell was accelerating the drift away from the grass roots which had begun with the Kilmainham Treaty. When violence flared up again in 1886, Parnell – fearing the effect on the Liberal alliance – immediately disassociated himself from it. Though his moderate supporters approved, more extreme nationalists became increasingly disillusioned. Tactically, like the Kilmainham Treaty, this may have been wise; strategically, the separation of the constitutional from the revolutionary movement was fatal to the cause of Home Rule. But for the moment this weakness was concealed.

In April 1887 *The Times* published (in facsimile) a letter which was supposed to have been written by Parnell, and in which he was alleged to have condoned the Phoenix Park Murders. Other revelations followed. When Parnell demanded a parliamentary investigation to clear his name, the Conservative government appointed a Special Judicial Commission charged with investigating the whole history of the past ten years. Parnell had to defend his entire record. After a year of searching investigation, the letters were shown to be forgeries. The Commission's Report, though it found that Parnell and his colleagues had promoted agrarian agitation, and had incited their followers to intimidate those who disagreed with them, dismissed all the serious charges. 'Well, really, between ourselves,' said Parnell, 'I think it is just about what I would have said myself.' The verdict raised him to a new peak of popularity. It seemed only a matter of time before he became the head of Ireland's first Home Rule government.

And then, in December 1889, came disaster. Captain William O'Shea, one of Parnell's former party colleagues, entered divorce proceedings against his wife, citing Parnell as co-respondent. Parnell, who believed that O'Shea could be bought off with a share of his wife's fortune, assured his colleagues that his reputation would not be damaged, and they (with the precedent of *The Times* letters in mind) believed him. But when the case came to court in November 1890 it at once became public knowledge what some had known for years – that Parnell and Katherine O'Shea had been lovers for nearly ten years, that Mrs O'Shea had borne Parnell's children and that since 1886 they had been living together as man and wife. The whole future of the Liberal-Nationalist alliance was threatened. The influential nonconformist supporters of the Liberal

The emotions roused by this split continued beyond Parnell's death. The legend grew of a great Irish leader rejected and destroyed by the ignorant populace at the bidding of the Liberal party and the Catholic Church. It was a legend immortalised by James Joyce in his book *A Portrait of the Artist as a Young Man*. Smouldering over the Christmas dinner table, the bitter wrangling between Dante and Mr Casey finally explodes:

'Devil out of hell! We won! We crushed him to death! Fiend!

The door slammed behind her.

Mr Casey, freeing his arms from his holders, suddenly bowed his head on his hands with a sob of pain.

Poor Parnell! he cried loudly. My dead king!'

party were outraged. Gladstone publicly warned the Irish party that they must choose between Parnell and Home Rule. If they chose Parnell his own leadership would become 'almost a nullity'. After a week of agonising debate the Irish party divided, and the majority chose the policy and not the man.

A majority chose the policy, but the man refused to surrender. The fight was carried to Ireland, where it continued for another eleven months in an increasing crescendo of bitterness. Parnell lost the support of the priests, for the Catholic Church could hardly condone adultery. He lost the support of the people, who could not see how Home Rule could be achieved without Liberal support. But he refused to accept defeat. And then, in October 1891, he died. He was only 45.

ULSTER WILL FIGHT

'In no spot in Europe has the French Revolution been celebrated with more splendour, seriousness and feeling than in the town of Belfast – if we except the very country where that astonishing event took place.'

At the end of the eighteenth century, Belfast had indeed been a stronghold of republican politics and religious tolerance. On 12 July 1784 the – exclusively Protestant – Volunteers paraded for mass at the opening of the first Catholic church in Belfast. In 1791, of course, the Society of United Irishmen had been founded in Belfast, and it was on Cave Hill (which towers over the city) that Wolfe Tone and his comrades had taken a solemn oath 'never to desist in our efforts until we have subverted the authority of England over our country and asserted her independence'.

And yet, by 1914, the city had become the headquarters of the Ulster Unionist Council, an organisation which had raised an army of 100,000 men, and established a provisional government determined to use 'all means which may be found necessary to defeat the present conspiracy to set up a Home Rule parliament in Ireland'. And in 1914 the Ulster Unionist Labour Association declared: 'We are prepared to die fighting for our freedom, for our birthright of British citizenship under British administration'.

The true extent of the change should not be exaggerated however. In the first place, the character of the French Revolution – as it developed during the 1790s – produced among Belfast liberals (as among liberals elsewhere) a reaction against revolutionary philosophy. Secondly, Protestant radicals in late eighteenth-century Belfast, however friendly to Catholics, had no doubt that an independent Ireland would be governed by people like themselves. In 1784, the town meeting passed a resolution declaring 'that the gradual extension of the suffrage to our long oppressed brethren the Roman Catholics, preserving unimpaired the Protestant government of this country, would be a measure fraught with the happiest consequences'. And, outside Belfast, competition for land, and the consequent dispossession of many Protestant tenants in favour of Catholics prepared to pay higher rents, had led, first to increasing violence between rival gangs of Protestant Peep o' Day Boys and Catholic Defenders, and then to the foundation of the Orange Order in County Armagh in 1795.

The same kind of reservations apply – though with rather less force – to the early twentieth century. Although there was always an articulate minority of Protestants in the north who supported Home Rule, they were always a minority. In 1905 Robert Lindsay Crawford tried to establish a new and non-sectarian Independent Orange Institution 'to bridge the gulf that has so long divided Ireland into hostile camps', but although the movement had some success at first, by 1910 the attempt had collapsed. The vast majority of the Protestant population in the north would have agreed with the Belfast man who said to me: 'In those days we didn't know exactly what Home Rule entailed, but we did know enough to know that it was something we shouldn't have'.

There were three main reasons for the development of such overwhelming resistance in the North even to the very limited independence that Home Rule would have given Ireland: an economic reason – industrialisation; a religious reason – mistrust of the Roman Catholic church; and a political reason – the fear of being overwhelmed in a Dublin parliament by a Nationalist majority.

In the first place, it was industrialisation which, more than anything else, helped to make the north – and especially Belfast – different from the rest of Ireland. By the end of the nineteenth century well over three quarters of Irish industry was concentrated in the Belfast area and this included two industries – linen and shipbuilding – as big as any in the United Kingdom. With few exceptions, industry outside the north was not concentrated in any one area, and it was organised largely in small firms serving a local market. Many in the north consequently despised the relatively underdeveloped south, and believed that Home Rule would mean their being dragged down to the inferior level of the rest of the country.

As we have seen, the linen industry was already well established in the north of Ireland by the end of the eighteenth century, though it was based largely in the countryside. It was also very much a domestic industry: linen was still spun and woven by hand. Bleaching and finishing were already factory processes however, though because both used water power, both were concentrated in the river valleys, and especially in the Lagan Valley above Belfast. This had led to the emergence of a substantial class of bleachers and drapers who dominated the industry and whose wealth was the foundation for its later development.

It was not linen however, but cotton which brought the industrial revolution to Ireland. Cotton spinning had begun in Belfast in 1777. The tariff protection which the Irish Parliament gave to Irish industries after the 'Constitution of 1782' and the prosperity created by the Napoleonic Wars started a substantial boom. As steam power was essential for the new industry this led to its concentration in Belfast. By 1815 there were 15 cotton mills in the city employing several thousand people; one had 300 workers. But the depression which followed the Napoleonic Wars, and the increasing competition from the very much stronger Lancashire cotton industry (especially after the removal of the protective duties in 1824) hit the infant industry very hard. By 1838 there were only five cotton spinning mills left in Belfast.

By chance a way was found out of this apparent impasse. In 1828, Thomas Mulholland's Belfast cotton mill was burnt down. 'Before rebuilding the mill, the question was discussed whether it should be adapted for spinning cotton as before, or for spinning flax or wool, and after giving the matter great consideration, and having collected much information on the subject, it was decided that as the English and Scottish competition in the cotton-spinning business was so great, and as the linen trade was the natural business of Ireland, it would be advisable in rebuilding the mill to adapt it for the spinning of flax by machinery, which was accordingly done.'

It was an immediate success; the new wet spinning process for linen, discovered in 1825, could produce much finer yarn and could spin much more consistently than was ever possible by hand, and by 1852 there were 28 flax spinning mills in the city. Some were very large – Mulhollands, for example, had 800 workers and 16,000 spindles, as many as the whole Belfast cotton industry in 1815. As many who could no longer make a living in the countryside crowded into Belfast to work in the new mills the city began to grow very rapidly – from about 20,000 in 1800 to 37,000 in 1821, 53,000 in 1831 and 70,000 in 1841.

Though linen spinning had become a factory industry, weaving was still done largely by hand. Handloom weaving had survived because it was cheap, but with the dramatic fall in population after the famine, wages rose 25 per cent in five years.

'So long as a man's labour could be had at the handloom in Ireland for a shilling a day, it was felt no powerloom could work much, if at all, cheaper; but when wages, some few years back, began to advance, and the population to decrease instead of increase, it was admitted that the power-loom was at length required.' Even so, because of early problems in weaving very fine linen on machinery, the power loom was slow to displace the handloom weaver – the number of spindles doubled between 1841 and 1861 to 593,000, but there were still less than 5,000 power-looms weaving linen in 1861.

It was the American civil war, which cut off Britain's cotton supplies, which finally launched the linen industry into full-scale industrial development. Between 1861 and 1868 the number of spindles rose from 593,000 to 894,000, the number of power-looms from 4933 to 12,969,[1] while the labour force increased by 70 per cent. And the industry became concentrated in and around Belfast: by 1870 80 per cent of the spindles and 70 per cent of the looms were in the Belfast area. The city's population continued to increase rapidly – 87,000 in 1851, 121,000 in 1861, 174,000 in 1871.

[1] As the problems of weaving fine linen by machinery were overcome, the number of power looms increased – there were 31,000 by 1900; but the number of spindles hardly increased at all.

The linen industry continued to prosper after the cotton industry had recovered in the mid-1870s, but two factors began increasingly to operate against it. Firstly, it did not have a large home market and was heavily dependent on exports, especially to the United States. The growth of tariff barriers in many overseas markets in the last quarter of the nineteenth century was therefore a growing anxiety. As it grew in scale the industry also became increasingly dependent on imported flax. Secondly, linen came under increasing competition from cotton, which was cheaper to produce, and easier to develop for the mass market; linen got the reputation of being a luxury. As one leading manufacturer said at the turn of the century: 'In my younger days, no one calling himself a gentleman wore anything but linen shirts; now but few do so. . . . Then, no ladies used anything but linen handkerchiefs; now, cotton handkerchiefs are sold in enormous quantities'.

The industry was also heavily dependent on the labour of women and young people. In 1890 70 per cent of the workers were women and 25 per cent boys and girls under 18. They worked long hours for low pay in 'dirty, disagreeable and dangerous conditions', but changes were resisted by the employers on the grounds that 'much more of this paternal legislation will have the tendency to legislate the trade out of the country'.

In Belfast, the main source of employment for men became shipbuilding. The industry was a major factor in the city's continuing prosperity and one in which the British connection was very important. Like many other small Irish ports Belfast had always built a few wooden ships, but the first permanent shipyard was established by William Ritchie, a Scot, in 1791. By 1812 he had launched 32 ships and was employing more than 100 men; in 1820 he launched the *Belfast*, one of the first steamships built in Ireland. In 1838 Victor Coates & Co., a firm of Belfast boilermakers, launched the first iron ship in Ireland, the *Countess of Caledon*. Until the second half of the century, however, shipbuilding in Belfast was no more significant than in half a dozen other Irish ports.

Indeed before there could be any large scale expansion of shipbuilding in Belfast the port itself needed drastic improvement. Until the 1840s bigger ships had to anchor two miles out in Belfast Lough and offload their cargoes into smaller boats. But in 1849 the Belfast Harbour Commissioners, founded two years earlier, completed a new deep water channel between the city and Belfast Lough. It was the first of a series of improvements which were still continuing fifty years later and which laid the foundation of Belfast's future prosperity.

The spoil from the new cut created a new island, which was named Queens Island. It was here, in 1858, that E. J. Harland, a Yorkshireman who had served his apprenticeship with the great locomotive engineer Robert Stephenson, took over a shipyard which the Harbour Commissioners had laid out five years before. He invited G. W. Wolff to join him, and four years later the two men became partners. Fifty years later, in a country with no iron and steel and virtually no coal, Harland and Wolff had become the largest shipyard in the world. A workforce of 500 men, who had launched a few thousand tons in 1860, had grown by 1910 to 12,000 and the yards' output had reached 116,000 tons.

Their success was based on the building of liners, first for the Bibby Line (one of whose directors, G. G. Schwabe, was Wolff's uncle) and then for the White Star Line, culminating between 1910 and 1914 in the *Olympic*, the *Titanic* and the *Britannic*, three of the largest ships in the world. As a contemporary authority, Professor Charles Oldham, said, Harland and Wolff 'have been pioneer builders of vessels of great size and of a new type, which were a great advance in marine construction and have largely revolutionised the conditions of ocean transport'.

Harland was the first shipbuilder to realise that the way in which wooden ships were built was not necessarily the best way to build iron ships; if iron ships were increased in length and strengthened by iron decks but without a corresponding increase being made in their beam, then, in Harland's own words: 'I conceived that they would show improved qualities in a sea way and that notwithstanding the increased accommodation the same speed with the same power would be obtained by only a slight increase in the first cost'.

Harland was proved right. In 1870 the *Oceanic*, built on these lines, achieved record speeds with a considerable reduction in fuel consumption – which meant of course that she could carry considerably more cargo. The *Oceanic* was also the first liner to have its first class accommodation amidships, and was consequently far more comfortable. The *Oceanic* was 400 feet long, 40 feet wide, and just over 4000 tons: the *Olympic* and the *Titanic*, launched 40 years later, were 850 feet long, 90 feet wide and 45,000 tons.

The company's achievements in marine engineering were equally significant. In 1880 Harland and Wolff set up their own engine works where they developed the twin screw, the triple and quadruple expansion engines, and the steam turbine, and finally the successful combination of the low-pressure turbine and the high-pressure reciprocal engine – 'a veritable inspiration of brainy ingenuity'.[2]

Though the industry appeared to be at a peak of prosperity in 1914, shipbuilding in Belfast, like linen, was increasingly vulnerable – and for the same reasons. Like linen, it imported all its raw materials. True, the higher cost of building ships in Belfast was offset by specialisation, and the higher labour costs of building passenger liners were offset by lower wage rates in Belfast. But all the ships were sold either in Britain or abroad, and they were increasingly threatened by foreign competition.

Industry in Belfast had developed as an integral part of the British economy, as the third angle of a triangle whose other angles were Liverpool and Glasgow. If Belfast were detached from Britain its industry would collapse. For both linen and shipbuilding the British connection was vital to their prosperity.

The continuing growth of Belfast at the end of the nineteenth century was based on the growth of the shipbuilding industry, whose output doubled between 1891 and 1914. The city's population, 174,999 in 1871, grew to 208,000 in 1881, 273,000 in 1891, 349,000 in 1901 and 386,000 in 1911. But the city's continued growth brought its own problems. Though new houses were built at an ever increasing rate – 4000 a year by the 1890s – and though many of these were built to the higher standards demanded by law after 1878, many appalling slums remained. 'To give accommodation to the thousand operatives which the giant demand of an unusually prosperous manufacture created', reported A. G. Malcolm in 1852, 'strings of houses on the simplest plan were hurried up, generally without sufficient carefulness as to drainage, ventilation, house wants or situation'; most of them were still lived in fifty years later.

And the city expanded too fast to provide its increasing population with adequate services. There was no proper sewage disposal system in the city until 1887, and no proper water supply until 1901. In 1851 the average life expectancy at birth was 9 years, and half the population of Belfast was under 20. Conditions improved in the next fifty years, but in 1897 27,000 people died of typhoid, and in 1906 an official report said: 'For the last 25 years at least, the mean annual mortality from typhoid fever has been so great in Belfast that no city or town of the United Kingdom equals or even approaches it in this respect'.

More significant than the simple growth of numbers in Belfast was the increase in the Catholic population. In 1800 only 1 in 10 of the city's 20,000 people was a Catholic. By 1861 1 in every 3 of the inhabitants – 41,000 out of 121,000 – was a Catholic, and though the proportion of Catholics then began to fall, there were still nearly 100,000 Catholics in Belfast in 1901 out of a population of 350,000.

And more important than the increase in the Catholic population was the fact that most of the city's new inhabitants were crowded into west Belfast. Already, by the middle of the nineteenth century, segregation between Catholics and Protestants was firmly established. Already, more than a hundred years ago, the

---

[2] Though Harland and Wolff dominated the industry, there was also Workman and Clark, known as 'the wee yard', though by 1910 it was the fourth largest in the United Kingdom and had pioneered the building of specialised cargo ships.

This map indicates the distribution of Roman Catholics, Presbyterians and Episcopalians (Church of Ireland) in Belfast according to the census of 1951. It is simplified to show the areas of greatest concentration of each of the three denominations. This understates the degree to which the population of Belfast is still segregated on religious lines, since the concentration of Catholics in areas where they are in a majority is very high – much higher than in Protestant areas. It is also noticeable how Presbyterians tend to be concentrated in residential, and Episcopalians in industrial, areas.

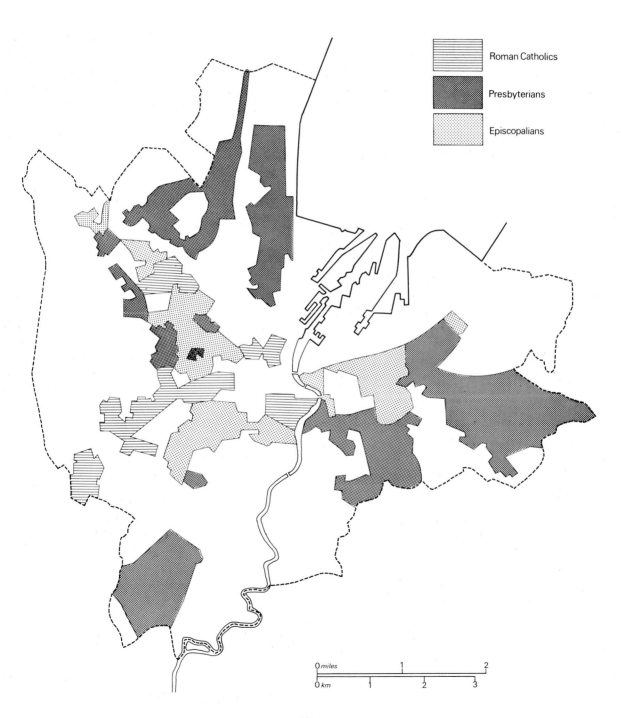

Roman Catholics

Presbyterians

Episcopalians

0 miles   1   2

0 km   1   2   3

Catholic Falls Road was flanked on one side by the Protestant Shankill Road and on the other by the Protestant Sandy Row. 'The people of the artisan and labouring classes,' said an official report in 1886, 'dwell to a large extent in separate quarters, each of which is given up almost entirely to persons of one particular faith, and the boundaries of which are sharply defined.'

It was religion which was the second major reason for the development of strong separatist feeling in the north, especially in Belfast. And yet, at the end of the eighteenth century, Belfast had been remarkable for its religious tolerance. Even as late as 1831 there were Protestants prepared to suscribe to the building of a new Catholic church in Belfast and to attend its first mass. That however was about the end of the line; the first serious sectarian riot took place four years later.[3] Thereafter, clashes between Catholics and Protestants began to recur with monotonous and sickening regularity; there were serious riots again in 1843, 1857, 1864, 1872, 1884, 1886, and 1898.

It was O'Connell's Emancipation campaign which began the change of mood. The way the campaign was run, the close involvement of the priests, the mass movement of Catholic peasantry created by the campaign, all suggested to both Catholics and Protestants that Catholics were the Irish Nation. This was not O'Connell's conscious intention, but it was certainly the effect – as Protestants in Belfast complained: 'A large proportion of the inhabitants of this island have been trained to regard us with unfriendly feelings as aliens and intruders'.

After this most Protestants saw Repeal as a direct threat to their position. When O'Connell came to Belfast in 1841 he had a hostile reception and had to be escorted out of town by a large police guard. At a protest meeting, a leading Presbyterian minister, the Rev. Henry Cooke declared: 'Repeal is but another name for Rebellion and a flimsy cover for the contemplated dismemberment of the Empire'.

Cooke was an extreme Calvinist of strong anti-Catholic views who had emerged victorious in a struggle with more liberal members of the church led by the Rev. Hugh Montgomery. 'Be watchful against the insidious advances of Popish error and despotism' he warned. 'Be united in defence of liberty and truth; and he who ruleth King of nations will bless and prosper your cause.' Cooke had considerable influence in the Presbyterian church and many others shared his views, notably the Rev. Hugh Hanna, who wrote: 'The design of Rome is to impose on her disciples an impossible rule, to paralyse the laity, to prevent the detection of her errors, to cast down in abject serfdom beneath the feet of a crafty and unscrupulous priesthood'.

The Church of Ireland had also been influenced by the evangelical movement of the 1830s and 1840s, and several of its clergy were equally vehement in their anti-Catholicism. One, the Rev. Thomas Drew, was held partly responsible for the riots of 1857. Drew was also the author of *Twenty Reasons for being an Orangeman*, one of which was: 'I learn by the doctrines, history and daily practices of the Church of Rome that the lives of Protestants are endangered, the laws of England set at naught, and the Crown of England subordinated to the dictates of an Italian bishop'. It was the Orange Order which the official enquiry held largely to blame for the 1857 disturbances. Though the Order had declined after 1815, Catholic Emancipation had revived it and the Order was very active in the 1820s and 1830s. Although, as the result of a parliamentary enquiry, the Grand Lodge of Ireland was dissolved in 1836, the Order survived in the north and its demonstrations continued. Sometimes these resulted in violence – as at Dolly's Brae in 1849, and again in 1864 when O'Connell was burned in effigy in Belfast after his memorial statue had been dedicated in Dublin.

The anti-Catholic views, both of the more vociferous clergy and of the Orange Order, appeared to many northern Protestants to be increasingly justified by events – by the growing influence of Catholic priests and bishops; by their enthusiastic involvement first with the Repeal campaign and later with the Home

---

[3] The first sectarian riot seems to have been in 1812-13 when it was believed Catholic Emancipation was imminent.

A Parliamentary Game of Shuttlecock

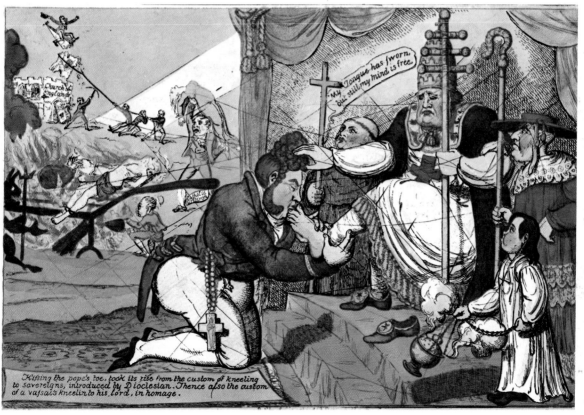

Page 50: a contemporary propaganda view of the Clare by-election in 1828 – The Speaker of the House of Commons preparing to use the Oath of Allegiance (his racket) to prevent O'Connell (on the shuttlecock) from taking his seat in the Commons (top) and O'Connell and his followers waiting for Emancipation to loose the dragon of persecution on Protestant heretics (bottom). Page 51: two similar views of the consequences of Catholic Emancipation – O'Connell Wellington and members of his government prepare to destroy the Church of England (top) whilst George IV kisses the Pope's foot, English Protestants are tortured as heretics (bottom).

Two cartoons from United Ireland *(a weekly Nationalist paper published in Dublin) commenting on Lord Randolph Churchill's visit to Belfast in February 1886.* King Randolph crossing the Boyne *(right) and* Beating the Orange Drum *(below). The grotesque faces of Churchill's Belfast audience show how Nationalist cartoonists also caricatured their opponents.*

Four cartoons from the Weekly Freeman (another Dublin Nationalist paper) commenting on the supposed influence of the Land League
(bottom right) and on the events of 1885–6. Gladstone (top left)
tramples his Unionist opponents (Lord Randolph Churchill is under
his sword), John Bull (top right) contemplates the sweeping
Nationalist victory at the polls, and the Lord Lieutenant (bottom left)
peers out of Dublin Castle at Parnell's triumphant reception in the
city.

Below: a few examples of the considerable output of Unionist propaganda during the Ulster crisis of 1911–14. On the left, two comments on the anticipated results of Home Rule – the destruction of Belfast's prosperity (top) and the incapacity of those farther south to govern themselves (bottom). On the right, two gestures of defiance – adhesive labels with Carson's portrait (top) and a poster commemorating Covenant Day 1912, signed by the artist (bottom).

Page 55: two more examples of Unionist propaganda – a punning reference (top) to Bonar Law's role in the crisis (the Red Hand is, of course, the badge of the province of Ulster) and an attack (bottom) on the Liberal dependence on Nationalist votes after the 1910 election. Redmond (with the flag) is leading – from left to right – Asquith, Lloyd George and Winston Churchill by the nose.

Rule movement; by the apparent effect of the Fenian rising of 1867 on British policy towards Ireland, and by the ambiguous relationship between agrarian violence and the Nationalist party in Parliament. All this led to the widespread belief amongst Protestants, especially in the north, that any independent Irish government would be priest-dominated, that their civil and religious liberties would be threatened – that Home Rule would mean Rome Rule.

Finally, in the 1885 election, with the electorate trebled by franchise reform, the Nationalists not only won every seat in Ireland outside Ulster, except for Dublin University, they also won 17 of the 33 seats in Ulster itself. This was significant for two reasons. The extent of their victory encouraged Nationalists to believe that the opposition to Home Rule was greatly exaggerated, but the closeness of the result in Ulster (which continued at every election thereafter) only intensified the already well-established siege mentality of Unionists.

When Gladstone introduced the first Home Rule Bill in 1886, all the fears of northern Protestants were suddenly brought into focus. The summer of 1886 was marked by some of the worst rioting ever seen in Belfast, which lasted most of the summer, cost 32 lives and several hundred injuries, and caused £90,000 worth of damage. And the instinctive reaction, to resort to armed resistance, received powerful support. At the height of the crisis, before the Home Rule Bill had been defeated, the Rev. Hugh Hanna had declared: 'Every capable loyalist should be enrolled in a loyal defensive union to meet any emergency that may arise. Let captains of fifties and captains of tens be elected and their corps constructed to meet the day of danger'.

For the first time, political issues became the main element in the disturbances. It was this which was to prove the third and most significant of all the reasons for the Ulster crisis of 1911–14. Politics in Ireland became completely polarised between Unionists and Nationalists; the Liberals were virtually destroyed.

The political issue was not however confined to Ireland. In February 1886 the ambitious and aggresively independent Conservative MP Lord Randolph Churchill wrote to his friend James FitzGibbon, Lord Chief Justice of Ireland: 'I decided some time ago that if the GOM[4] went for Home Rule, the Orange card would be the one to play. Please God it may turn out the ace of trumps and not the two'. Later the same month he came to Ireland. At Larne he made a speech in which he used a phrase that was later to become famous – 'Ulster will fight and Ulster will be right', and in Belfast he called for Loyalists to 'wait and watch, organise and prepare', so that if the blow [Home Rule] came it should not come upon them 'as a thief in the night'. If it did, he declared, 'in that dark hour there will not be wanting those of position and influence in England who are willing to cast in their lot with you, whatever it may be, and who will share your fortune and your fate'. Partly this was an attempt to exploit Unionist anxieties in Ulster for the benefit of the Conservative party in Britain, but partly it was inspired by a genuine belief that Home Rule was a threat to the Empire, and to the integrity and security of the United Kingdom.

Perhaps the most important result of the events of 1886 was to make militant Unionism respectable. In the next few years, as Lord Cushendun later recalled: 'Large numbers of country gentlemen, clergymen of all Protestant denominations, business and professional men, farmers and the better class of artisans in Belfast and other towns joined the lodges[5] the management of which passed into capable hands; the Society was thereby completely and rapidly transformed and, instead of being a somewhat disreputable and obsolete survivor, it became a highly respectable as well as an exceedingly powerful political organisation'.

Gladstone's defeat over Home Rule in 1886 removed the immediate danger to the Unionist position, but the same symptoms reappeared when Gladstone returned to power in 1892. There was a huge Unionist convention in Belfast, attended by 12,000 representatives from all the Ulster constituencies, with an estimated crowd

[4] Grand Old Man – Gladstone.
[5] Of the Orange Order.

of 300,000 outside. It was here that the Duke of Abercorn raised his right arm and asked the audience to repeat solemnly after him 'We will not have Home Rule', and here that the audience leapt to their feet and cheered for several minutes when Thomas Andrews declared that 'as a last resort we will be prepared to defend ourselves'.

The defeat of the second Home Rule Bill in 1893 again removed the immediate threat, but the success of the conference which had prepared the way for the 1903 Land Act so impressed the landlords' representatives that they founded the Irish Reform Association to develop co-operation between moderates of all political parties. In September 1904 the Association put forward proposals for the limited devolution of power from Westminster to a council in Ireland. In the north, where there were strong (though completely unfounded) suspicions that this was an attempt by the Conservative party 'to grant Home Rule on the sly', the Unionist reaction in 1905 was to found the Ulster Unionist Council 'to revive on a war footing for active work the various Ulster defence associations'.

When the next crisis came in 1912, however, it was seen at once to be much more serious. Until then, any Home Rule Bill, even if got through the House of Commons (as the 1893 bill had done) was bound to be rejected by the large Unionist majority in the House of Lords. But, as a result of the great constitutional crisis precipitated by Lloyd George's 1909 budget and the two general elections of 1910, the Lords' veto was restricted, by the Parliament Act of 1911, to three sessions of Parliament. After the election of 1910, the Liberals depended for their majority – as Gladstone had depended in 1886 – on the support of the Irish Nationalists. In April 1912, Asquith, the Liberal Prime Minister, introduced the third Home Rule Bill. There was no reason, even if the Lords delayed it, why it should not become law in 1914.

Although the Bill conceded self-government only on purely Irish affairs and restricted all important matters – like defence and foreign policy – to Westminster, there was still, as in 1886, a nagging fear amongst Unionists that this would not be regarded in Ireland as a final settlement. Even the conservative leader of the Nationalist party, John Redmond, referred to the Bill as 'provisional' and looked forward to 'when the time for revision does come'.

For Unionist leaders, Home Rule remained a potential threat to civil and religious liberties, and to the integrity and security of the Empire. Their supporters were less concerned with constitutional niceties. For them the issue was simple: either to remain free and prosperous – as they thought they were – or to become enslaved and impoverished. But both leaders and rank and file were determined to oppose Home Rule by all the means in their power.

In opposing it, they were brilliantly led by the Dublin lawyer, Sir Edward Carson, who had become leader of the Irish Unionists in 1910; the campaign in Ulster was ably orchestrated by one of his fellow MPs, James Craig, and supported by generous contributions from Ulster businessmen. In September 1911, at a massive demonstration at Craig's house, Craigavon, near Belfast, Carson set the tone of the campaign. 'We must be prepared,' he said, 'in the event of a Home Rule Bill passing, with such measures as will carry on for ourselves the government of those districts of which we have control. We must be prepared, the morning Home Rule passes, ourselves to become responsible for the government of the Protestant province of Ulster'. Two days later, the Ulster Unionist Council in Belfast appointed a Commission of five leading local men 'to take immediate steps, in consultation with Sir Edward Carson, to frame and submit a constitution for a Provisional Government of Ulster . . . the powers and duration of such a Provisional Government to come into operation on the day of the passage of any Home Rule Bill, and to remain in force until Ulster shall again resume unimpaired her citizenship in the United Kingdom'.

The Unionists were greatly assisted in their campaign by the vociferous support they received from the Conservative party, and especially from its new leader, Andrew Bonar Law (whose family came originally from Ulster). He did not hesitate to commit his party to

ULSTER
PROVISIONAL GOVERNMENT

PROCLAMATION

TO ALL WHOM IT MAY CONCERN.

WHEREAS ULSTERMEN, Free Citizens of a United Kingdom, Born into Possession of Full Rights and Privileges under ONE KING and ONE IMPERIAL PARLIAMENT, are threatened with the calamity of being deprived of their Birthright and being Forcibly Subjected to a Nationalist Parliament and Executive, regardless of their steadfast allegiance in the past to their King and Empire,

BE IT KNOWN

That, for the Public Safety and Security of Civil and Religious Liberty to ALL Classes and Creeds, duly-elected Delegates and Covenanters representative of all parts of Ulster, in the City of Belfast this day assembled, finally settled the form of

PROVISIONAL GOVERNMENT

WITHIN THE PROVINCE OF ULSTER.

THE DATE upon which it shall become effective, together with instructions regarding all other matters necessary for Repudiating and Resisting the Decrees of such Nationalist Parliament or Executive and for taking over the Government of the Province IN TRUST for the British Nation will be made public as and when it shall be deemed expedient.

ON BEHALF OF THE CENTRAL AUTHORITY.

EDWARD CARSON.
LONDONDERRY.
ABERCORN.
JOHN YOUNG.
THOMAS SINCLAIR.
THOMAS ANDREWS.

OLD TOWN HALL, BELFAST, 24th SEPTEMBER, 1913.

GOD SAVE THE KING.

the most extreme positions. In April 1912, at another massive demonstration at the Balmoral showground in Belfast, he made a dramatic speech full of references to the siege of Londonderry in 1689. 'Once again you hold the pass, the pass for the Empire' he said. 'You are a beseiged city. The timid have left you; your Lundys have betrayed you; but you have closed your gates. The Government have erected by their Parliament Act a boom against you to shut you off from the help of the British people. You will burst that boom.[6] That help will come, and when the crisis is over, men will say to you in words not unlike those used by Pitt – you have saved yourselves by your exertions and you will save the Empire by your example.' In July, at a Unionist demonstration at Blenheim Palace – justifying the gravity of his language with the charge that the Liberals had no mandate for Home Rule and had made a corrupt parliamentary bargain with the Nationalists, he added: 'I can imagine no length of resistance to which Ulster can go in which I should not be prepared to support them, and in which, in my belief, they would not be supported by the overwhelming majority of the British people'.

During the summer of 1912 there were several serious outbreaks of sectarian violence. A Protestant Sunday School outing was attacked by Catholics at Castledawson, County Londonderry; reprisals were taken against Catholics in the Belfast shipyards; and serious fighting broke out at a football match between Celtic and Linfield – traditional sectarian rivals. The Unionist leaders needed both a safety valve for popular emotion and some convincing demonstration of the movement's self-discipline. It was accordingly announced that 28 September would be Ulster Day, when loyalists would 'pledge themselves to a solemn covenant'. At a series of preparatory meetings, beginning at Enniskillen on 10 September and ending with a great eve of Covenant rally in the Ulster Hall,

Belfast, Carson addressed the crowds and one resolution was passed: 'We will not have Home Rule'.

Finally, on 28 September 1912, after services of dedication all over the city, Carson led a huge procession to the City Hall in Belfast to sign the Covenant, pledging all who signed it 'to stand by one another in defending for ourselves and our children our cherished position of equal citizenship in the United Kingdom, and in using all means which may be found necessary to defeat the present conspiracy to set up a Home Rule Parliament in Ireland'. The vast crowd was admitted in batches of 400–500 at a time; 150 signed the Covenant every minute; and the signing went on until 11 o'clock at night. J. L. Garvin, of the *Observer*, was watching from City Hall. 'No one for a moment could have mistaken the concentrated will and courage of these people' he said. 'They do not know what fear and flinching mean in this business, and they are not going to know. They do not, indeed, believe it possible that they can be beaten.' All over Ulster the scene was repeated on a smaller scale. 471,414 people signed the Covenant that day, some of them in their own blood.

The logical end of all this was violence, for if the Unionists really meant what they said, then their resistance to Home Rule might indeed have to be a protest in arms. The law allowed any two JP's to authorise drilling and other military operations in their areas for the defence of the realm, and in 1912 some Unionists, especially in the Orange Order, used this legal anomaly to organise para-military groups. At their annual meeting in January 1913, the Ulster Unionist Council decided that all these activities should be brought together in one body, to be known as the Ulster Volunteer Force. 90,000 men were enrolled and organised into regiments and battalions, with a number of specialised corps – cavalry, medical and nursing, motor cars, signallers and despatch riders. The whole force was run by an experienced headquarters staff of retired professional soldiers led by Lieutenant-General Sir George Richardson, a veteran of the Afghan Wars.

Though there had been a fair amount of smuggling, and some arms and ammunition had reached Ulster,

[6] Lundy – still a synonym for traitor in Northern Ireland – was the name of the governor of Londonderry who was prepared to surrender the city to the forces of James II, which later tried to starve the city into submission by placing a boom across the river Foyle.

Ulster's
Solemn League and Covenant.

Being convinced in our consciences that Home Rule would be disastrous to the material well-being of Ulster as well as of the whole of Ireland, subversive of our civil and religious freedom, destructive of our citizenship and perilous to the unity of the Empire, we, whose names are underwritten, men of Ulster, loyal subjects of His Gracious Majesty King George V., humbly relying on the God whom our fathers in days of stress and trial confidently trusted, do hereby pledge ourselves in solemn Covenant throughout this our time of threatened calamity to stand by one another in defending for ourselves and our children our cherished position of equal citizenship in the United Kingdom and in using all means which may be found necessary to defeat the present conspiracy to set up a Home Rule Parliament in Ireland. ¶ And in the event of such a Parliament being forced upon us we further solemnly and mutually pledge ourselves to refuse to recognise its authority. ¶ In sure confidence that God will defend the right we hereto subscribe our names. ¶ And further, we individually declare that we have not already signed this Covenant.

in my own blood

The above was signed by me at _The City Hall Belfast_ at "Ulster Day," Saturday, 28th September, 1912. 3-45 pm

Fred H. Crawford _Chlorine Gardens &
20 mill st Belfast_

———— God Save the King. ————

the UVF had mostly to drill with dummy weapons. In January 1914, therefore, Major Fred Crawford, an experienced arms smuggler, was asked by Unionist leaders to organise the purchase, transport and landing of a substantial quantity of weapons. On the night of 24 April 1914, under cover of a test mobilisation of the UVF, and while a convincing diversion was staged in Belfast, Crawford in the SS *Clydevalley* landed 25,000 German rifles and 2 million rounds of ammunition at Larne, Bangor and Donaghadee. The cargo was distributed with remarkable speed and efficiency all over Ulster before the authorities knew anything about the operation. As Lord Roberts said: 'It was a piece of organisation that any army in Europe might be proud of'.

The British government was now faced with the real possibility of armed resistance. Even before this, the Liberals had found it impossible to coerce the Unionists into accepting Home Rule. In March 1914 a number of British army officers in Ireland had indicated that they would rather resign their commissions than move against Ulster – the so-called Curragh incident.

The Liberals had in fact always been dubious about the justice – let alone the wisdom – of coercion. As early as February 1912 the Cabinet had decided to make concessions to the Unionists if this proved absolutely necessary. In June 1912, the Hon. T. G. R. Agar-Robartes, the Liberal member for St Austell, had moved an amendment to the Home Rule Bill to exclude its operation in the four north-eastern counties – Antrim, Down, Armagh and Londonderry. The Unionists, unwilling to appear intransigent (and believing in any case that the exclusion of these four counties would wreck any Home Rule regime in Dublin) supported the amendment. Already however they were beginning to consider the possibility that they might have to accept the exclusion of Ulster from any Home Rule Parliament, and that if so, this should be the largest possible area consistent with preserving a comfortable Protestant majority. This led to an increasing divergence of interest between Unionists in the north, where there was a large Protestant population from all classes of society, and Unionists in the south, who were a scattered and privileged minority.

Between October 1913 and January 1914, Asquith and Bonar Law met several times to investigate whether, and if so how, Ulster could be excluded from the Home Rule Bill. In March 1914, moving the third reading of the Bill in the Commons, Asquith announced that the government was prepared to allow any Ulster county to opt out of the jurisdiction of a Home Rule Parliament for six years. Though the Nationalists were resolutely opposed to partition in any form, Redmond was persuaded to accept the temporary exclusion of some Ulster counties. Carson however contemptuously rejected the amendment. 'We do not want sentence of death', he said, 'with a stay of execution for six years.'

The Government persisted with its amendment, but in June – when the Bill went to the Lords for the last time – Unionist peers amended the Bill to allow for the permanent exclusion of the whole province of Ulster. As a result, later in the month, King George V called an all-party conference in the hope of resolving the deadlock. But it was impossible to get agreement either on what part of Ulster should be excluded or, if so, for how long this should be. After four days the conference broke down.

But if the Liberals could not coerce the Unionists into accepting the Home Rule Bill, neither could the Unionists prevent the Home Rule Bill becoming law. It seemed that civil war was inevitable.

The Buckingham Palace Conference broke down on 24 July 1914. Within a week, Irish affairs – which had seemed so important for nearly three years – became no more than a minor episode in the shadow of a larger and infinitely more terrible struggle. As Winston Churchill recalled: 'The parishes of Fermanagh and Tyrone faded back into the mists and squalls of Ireland, and a strange light began immediately, but by perceptible gradations, to fall and grow upon the map of Europe'. On 4 August 1914, Britain was at war with Germany.

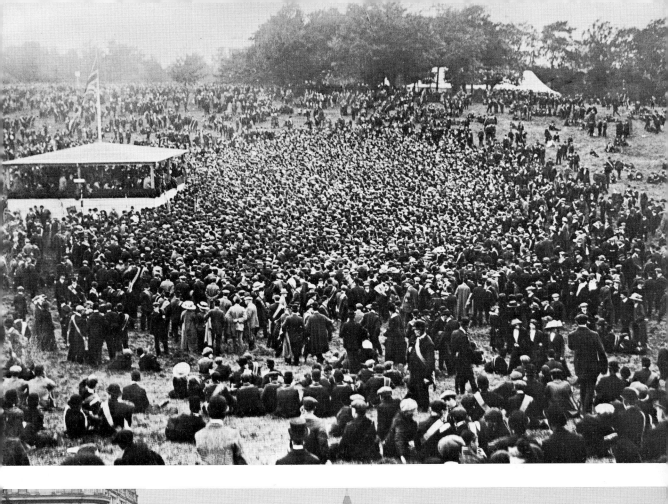

Top: a detachment of the UVF drilling, in the early days after its formation, with wooden rifles – perhaps those sold by a Belfast firm 'shaped as nearly as possible like a service weapon, at one shilling and eightpence each in pitch pine, or one shilling and sixpence in spruce'.

Bottom: Carson inspects the West Belfast regiment of the UVF a Glencairn on 6 June 1914, a few weeks after the Larne gun-running 'I rely on every man', said Carson, 'to fight for his arms – and let no man take them from him'.

Two of a series of propaganda postcards issued in Belfast after the gun-running: The motors on the way to Larne *(top)* and Unloading the guns at Donaghadee *(bottom)*. *The efficiency with which the several hundred vehicles were assembled, loaded and des-* patched with their canvas bundles of weapons was one of the most remarkable features of the whole operation. Craig was in charge of the unloading at Donaghadee, which had to be done in broad daylight – 'police, coastguards and customs looking on, but not interfering'.

The Ulster Scot

This land oor heritage by richt

Priest ridden saints may grudge us

Three hunner years we hae been here

AN DEIL TH' FIT

THEY'LL BUDGE US

Three of the considerable number of propaganda postcards of the 1911-1914 period (see also page 54). The Ulster Scot is an interesting assertion of the equal right of Scots Presbyterians to the land of Ireland. Below, two views of Carson – the Hero of the Union, *with a suitably defiant verse, and the fanatic with delusions of grandeur, who cannot achieve success by his chosen method.*

ULSTER'S SOLEMN COVENANT

SIR EDWARD CARSON

HEROES OF THE UNION

Behind this gallant Statesman are men who lead the cause.
The glorious cause of Union. Men of Ulster! do not pause.
We have signed the Solemn Covenant, which binds us to defend
Our faith, our flag, our loyalty unflinching to the end.

OH! WHAT A FALL THERE'LL BE.

Carson clinging staunch
To a weak and falling branch,
Thinks he'll saw a way out of Home Rule;
And he'll never, never stop,
'Till he gets an awful drop;
For he works with an impossible tool

66

GREEN, WHITE AND GOLD

For five days, at Easter 1916, about 1600 men had held out in the GPO, and other selected strongholds in Dublin, against the superior numbers and equipment of the British army. Few outside the inner circle who who had planned the Rising had expected it. Fewer still, either in Dublin or the world beyond, realised that it would have such profound consequences. For less than two years later the Irish Nationalist party, which had dominated Irish political life for more than thirty years, was annihilated at the election of December 1918. The 73 Sinn Fein members who replaced them refused to take their seats in the British House of Commons and established an alternative government in Ireland. And, in December 1921, after two years of bitter guerilla warfare, and less than five years after an insurrection which had appeared to many at the time to be a ridiculous farce, the British government – which had for so long refused to contemplate anything of the kind – agreed to the establishment of the Irish Free State.

It is easy for us looking back now to suppose that what happened in Ireland between 1916 and 1921 was inevitable. It is equally easy to see, in the perspective of history, the various features of Irish society in the years before 1916 that made these events possible. It is more difficult to realise that, certainly in April 1916 and perhaps even later, what happened in Ireland between 1916 and 1921 was far from inevitable, and that the major features of Irish society in the years before 1916 were its growing prosperity and apparent political stability.

Parnell's death did not heal the split in the parliamentary party; indeed the quarrel continued even during the debate on the second Home Rule Bill in 1893. The division of the party into Parnellites and anti-Parnellites persisted for a further seven years, and for most of this time the anti-Parnellites were also divided amongst themselves. 'We are torn by internal dissensions', said Justin McCarthy in 1894, 'and, all the while, some of us have to keep up a good appearance in the more or less futile hope of concealing from the world the true and ominous story of our trouble.'

Finally, in 1900, the split was patched up, and the party reunited under the leadership of the Parnellite John Redmond. 'In the name of Ireland', resolved the members of the various factions, 'we declare at an end the divisions which hitherto separated the Irish Nationalist representatives and we hereby form ourselves into one united party.'

But though formally the discipline, the unity and the independence of the party were re-established, the party never again became the cohesive force it had been in the 1880s. Party discipline was much looser, a small but articulate group of members split off from the party and sat as independents, and – above all – Home Rule depended, as it had done ever since 1886, on the goodwill of the Liberal party. But the Liberal party was out of office between 1895 and 1905, and between 1906 and 1910 the Liberals had such a large majority that they had no need of Nationalist support. Nevertheless, throughout this period the Nationalist party commanded the loyalty of the vast majority of the Irish people, and in spite of occasional, though temporary, electoral set-backs, the Nationalist strength in the House of Commons never fell below 80 MPs. But the party's single-minded commitment to Home Rule, and the failure of most of its members to recognise the significance of the new ideas that were increasingly attracting younger men, began to undermine its authority.

Some of the elements in this newer and more aggressive nationalism had begun to appear even before Parnell's death. In 1884 Michael Cusack had founded the Gaelic Athletic Association, to wean the youth of Ireland away from subservience to 'foreign' – that is British – games. The GAA spread rapidly, and within five years it had 50,000 members. It was remarkably successful both in developing a sense of Irish nationality and in encouraging local patriotism; at a time when the countryside was emptying fast, the GAA did more than almost anything else to maintain a sense of identity amongst those who remained. Perhaps more important even than this was the rejection of England that accompanied it. As Archbishop Croke of Cashel wrote to Cusack: 'If we continue travelling for the next score years in the same direction that we have been going in for some time past, condemning the sports that were practised by our forefathers, effacing our national features as though we were ashamed of them and putting on, with England's stuffs and broadcloths, her masher's habits, and such other effeminate follies as she may recommend, we had better at once, and publicly, abjure our nationality, clap hands for joy at the sight of the Union Jack, and place "England's bloody red" exultantly above the "Green".'

It is not surprising therefore that at least 4 of the 7 men who attended the Association's inaugural meeting were members of the IRB, and that the GAA rapidly became a nursery for extreme nationalists.

A more subtle and more powerful instrument in the development of a new sense of Irish nationality was the Gaelic League, founded in 1893. The League had two main objects – first 'the preservation of Irish as the National Language of Ireland and the extension of its use as a spoken tongue', and second 'the study and publication of existing Gaelic literature and the cultivation of a modern literature in Irish'. The League's first President was Douglas Hyde, a Protestant who believed that the movement should remain non-political, but who had also given a famous lecture in 1892 on *The Necessity for De-Anglicising Ireland*. 'In Anglicising ourselves wholesale', said Hyde, 'we have thrown away with a light heart the best claim which we have upon the world's recognition of us as a separate nationality', and he called on his audience to 'foster a native spirit and a growth of native custom which will form the strongest barrier against English influence and be in the end the surest guarantee of Irish autonomy.' The League grew rapidly – from 58 branches in 1898 to 900 in 1906 with 100,000 members, and for many young people the discovery of the Irish language was also the discovery of their Irish national identity.[1]

Pointing in the same direction, and ultimately of much greater importance than the Gaelic League, was Sinn Fein (Ourselves), an organisation based on the views of Arthur Griffith. Griffith became editor of the weekly *United Ireland* in March 1899, and made his position clear in the very first issue: 'Lest there might be a doubt in any mind, we will say that we accept the nationalism of '98, '48 and '67 as the true nationalism and Grattan's cry "Live Ireland – perish the Empire!" as the watch-word of patriotism'. Home Rulers might acknowledge England's right to govern their country, wrote Griffith, but 'the Nationalist on the other hand totally rejects the claim of England, or any other country, to rule over or interfere with the destinies of Ireland'. Though Griffith was an effective journalist however, he had less interest in political organisation and it was not until 1905 that Sinn Fein became a national organisation dedicated to 'the re-establishment of the independence of Ireland'. Even then it remained small and politically ineffective; although it won a few seats on the Dublin City Council and made a respectable showing at a by-election in North Leitrim in 1908, Sinn Fein failed to make much impact on the electorate and was almost defunct by 1910.

But Griffith's *ideas* were to have much more influence. The basis of his policy was national self-reliance – 'an Irish state governed by Irishmen for the benefit of the Irish people'. Instead of concentrating on agriculture, and being economically dependent on Britain for her manufactured goods, said Griffith, Ireland should develop her own industries behind protective tariff barriers; for without industrial development Ireland would never acquire any real political power. Politically, Griffith believed that Irish MPs should boycott the Westminster Parliament, refuse to recognise its right to legislate for Ireland, and establish a Parliament of their own – just as he believed the Hungarian deputies in the Austro-Hungarian Imperial Diet had done in 1861. Just as this had led – so Griffith believed – to the establishment of an independent Hungarian Parliament, so it would lead to the establishment of an independent Irish Parliament.

[1] I have concentrated here on the immediate political significance of the Gaelic revival. Its cultural achievements, its relationship with the Anglo-Irish literary renaissance and its influence on the country's political future are discussed in chapter 9 (pp. 114–121).

'Sixty years ago', he wrote, 'Hungary realised that the political centre of the nation must be within the nation. When Ireland realises this obvious truth and turns her back on London, the parallel may be completed.'

The most radical of the new developments – and the only one to involve large numbers of ordinary people – was the Labour movement. In 1908 Jim Larkin organised the Irish Transport and General Workers Union. In the years that followed he organised a series of strikes which, even though not all of them were successful, gave his members a new self-respect. In the summer of 1913 there was a long and bitter strike, first of Dublin tramway workers, and then of all the Union's members in the commercial empire of the wealthy industrialist, William Martin Murphy.[2] The strike developed into a lockout; there were several violent clashes between strikers and police, and on 31 August, when Larkin was trying to address a crowd in the centre of Dublin, the police turned on them with their batons. Two people were killed and many hundreds – including 200 policemen – wounded. As a result, the union established the Irish Citizen Army for its own protection.

In 1914, when Larkin left Ireland for America, his place was taken by James Connolly. In 1896, Connolly had founded the Irish Socialist Republican party, which looked forward to the establishment of a socialist republic in Ireland 'based upon the public ownership by the Irish people of the land and the means of production, distribution and exchange'.[3] In 1911 he had become Larkin's organiser in Belfast and had quickly established himself as the brains of the labour movement. Now he became the driving force behind both the Union and the Citizen Army. But though Connolly believed in a workers' republic, he believed equally strongly in national independence. 'The struggle for Irish freedom has two aspects', he wrote, 'it is national

and it is social. The national ideal can never be realised until Ireland stands forth before the world as a nation, free and independent. It is social and economic because, no matter what the form of government may be, as long as one class owns as private property the land and instruments of labour from which mankind derive their substance, that class will always have it in their power to plunder and enslave the remainder of their fellow creatures'.

Organised labour, Sinn Fein and the Gaelic League were all new movements, but in spite of its virtual eclipse after the New Departure, the Irish Republican Brotherhood – the Fenians – remained in existence. As a contemporary said, however, by the early years of this century, its members were doing little except 'sitting on their backsides and criticising and abusing one another'. These elderly and virtually retired revolutionaries, under whom the movement had been quietly going to seed for the last twenty years, were now gradually replaced by younger men – notably Denis McCullough, Bulmer Hobson (both Belfast men), and Sean MacDermott. Their aims, as Hobson described them, were the old straightforward republicanism of the Fenians: 'We stand for an Irish republic because we see that no compromise with England, no repeal of the Union, no concession of Home Rule, or Devolution, will satisfy the national aspirations of the Irish people. . . . National independence is our right; we ask no more and we will accept no less'. The new men owed much of their success in rejuvenating the movement to the wholehearted support of Tom Clarke, a member of the IRB's Supreme Council. Clarke was a fanatically committed Fenian who had spent 15 years in prison for his part in their bombing campaign in England in the early 1880s, and who returned to Dublin in 1907. But although the IRB was rejuvenated, it remained for the moment small, poor and ineffective. Its opportunity was to come, paradoxically, from the reaction – both in Britain and in Ulster – to the third Home Rule Bill.

After the constitutional crisis over the 1909 budget and the two general elections of 1910, Asquith, the

[2] Murphy had been a Nationalist MP and was the proprietor of the *Irish Independent*, a Nationalist newspaper. The conservatism of men like Murphy was one of the things which made the party increasingly unacceptable to radicals.
[3] The experiment was largely abortive, and Connolly spent seven years in America, only returning to Ireland in 1910.

Liberal prime minister, depended for his majority in the House of Commons on Irish Nationalist support and he had committed his government to Home Rule. When, in April 1912, he introduced the third Home Rule Bill into the House of Commons, it seemed that John Redmond and the Irish Nationalist party were about to reap the harvest of thirty years of constitutional agitation. 'If I may say so reverently', said Redmond, 'I personally thank God that I have lived to see this day. I believe the Bill will pass into law. I believe it will result in the greater unity and strength of the Empire. I believe it will put an end once and for all to the wretched ill-will, suspicion and disaffection that have existed in Ireland, and to the suspicion and misunderstanding that have existed between this country and Ireland.'

The great mass of the Irish people agreed with him. 'Ten years ago', complained *Irish Freedom*, the IRB's paper, 'the parliamentary party was losing its grip on the country . . . Today, the parliamentary party controls more thoroughly than ever the daily press and the public in Ireland . . . and the Irish people accept and applaud the betrayal of everything national they once professed to advocate.'

But the situation was radically altered by the extremely hostile Unionist reaction to the Bill, and above all by their enthusiastic support for Ulster's determined attempt to resist it. Redmond and his colleagues in the Nationalist party greatly underestimated both the strength and the violence of this resistance and the extent to which Unionists in Britain would support it. Indeed they persisted in regarding it as bluff long after the Liberal government had become seriously concerned about the possibility of an Ulster rebellion. 'We do not believe in the reality of the threats of civil war indulged in by Sir Edward Carson and his followers', said Joe Devlin – who sat for West Belfast – in February 1914, 'and we are convinced that the danger is grotesquely exaggerated'. Asquith did not share this view. Moreover, pressure on the Liberals for some kind of compromise over Ulster was increasing. Redmond might declare 'Irish Nationalists can never be assent-

ing parties to the mutilation of the Irish nation', but the Irish Nationalists had no way of putting pressure on the Liberal government to prevent it. Eventually, in March 1914, Asquith got Redmond to agree to the temporary exclusion of six Ulster counties from the operation of the Home Rule Bill – only to have the proposal contemptuously rejected by the Unionists. Almost immediately the Curragh 'mutiny' and the Larne gun-running made it appear increasingly likely that the issue could only be settled by force.

A significant body of opinion in Ireland had already reached the same conclusion. On 1 November 1913, Eoin MacNeill, a moderate and influential Ulster Catholic who had been the first secretary of the Gaelic League, wrote an article called 'The North began' in the League's paper *An Claidheamh Soluis*. In it he declared that the formation of the UVF was both an example and a warning to the rest of the country, because 'it was precisely with this object that the Volunteers of 1782 were enrolled, and they became the instrument of establishing Irish self-government'. At a public meeting in the Dublin Rotunda on 25 November MacNeill declared: 'In a crisis of this kind the duty of safeguarding our own rights is our first and foremost. They have rights who dare maintain them'; and he proposed the formation of the Irish Volunteers 'to secure and maintain the rights and liberties of *all* the people of Ireland'. Four thousand recruits were immediately enrolled, and by July 1914 the recruits were 160,000 strong – more than 40,000 of them in Ulster.

At the end of the month, in a coup even more daring than the Larne gun-running (since it took place in broad daylight), 1,500 rifles and 58,000 rounds of ammunition were landed at Howth and Kilcoole. This gun-running was largely the work of Protestant sympathisers with the Nationalist cause; the money was raised by a committee in London which included Sir Roger Casement; the arms were bought in Hamburg and brought over to Ireland in two yachts belonging to members of the Anglo-Irish gentry.

With the fate of the Home Rule Bill still in the balance, Redmond had become increasingly concerned

The seven men who signed the pro-clamation declaring the establishment of an Irish republic on Easter Monday 1916.
Left to right: Patrick Pearse, Joseph Plunkett, Eamonn Ceannt. Page 72: Thomas MacDonagh, Tom Clarke, Sean MacDermott, James Connolly.

during the early months of 1914 at the challenge presented by the Volunteers to the parliamentary party's authority. In June 1914 he therefore demanded – and obtained – 25 of his own nominees on the Provisional Committee, the governing body of the Volunteers. Having gained control of the movement, he then – when the Great War broke out – committed it to the defence of Ireland. On 3 August, in an emotional speech in the House of Commons, he said: 'We offer to the government of the day that they may take their troops away, and that, if it is allowed to us, in comradeship with our brethren in the north, we will ourselves defend the coasts of our country'. At first Redmond insisted that the Volunteers should not be required to fight overseas, but on 20 September, he spoke at a Volunteer review at Woodenbridge, Co Wicklow, calling on his audience to 'account yourselves as men, not only in Ireland itself, but wherever the firing line extends, in defence of right, of freedom and of religion in this war'.

At once the Volunteers split in two. Many agreed with Tom Kettle, a young Nationalist MP, that 'to counsel Ireland to stand neutral in judgement is as if one were to counsel a Christian to stand neutral in judgement between Nero and St Peter', and these men – about 170,000 of them – remained loyal to Redmond as the National Volunteers; many thousands later joined the British army. But a minority of about 11,000 repudiated Redmond's speech and broke away under MacNeill, retaining the name Irish Volunteers. The Home Rule Bill had finally become law on 18 September – but it was suspended until after the war and, more important, until it had been amended 'in such a way as to secure the general consent both of Ireland and of the United Kingdom'. Redmond believed that Ireland's contribution to the war effort would place Britain under a moral obligation to grant Home Rule after the war. MacNeill, on the other hand, wanted to keep the Volunteers in being – and in Ireland – to ensure that Home Rule for the whole island was indeed achieved after the war.

From the very beginning however the IRB had taken a close interest in the Volunteers. Bulmer Hobson had been largely responsible for organising the Rotunda meeting in September 1913, and later for planning the Howth gun-running. There had been 12 members of the IRB on the original Provisional Committee of 30 and the executive committee of the Irish Volunteers was now dominated by IRB men. And the IRB's Supreme Council had already decided that there should be an armed rising during the war.

But the preparations for this rising were not just the work of the IRB, but of a secret group *within* the IRB mining busily away inside the framework of the Volunteers. The members of this second group – the Military Committee – were Patrick Pearse, the Volunteer Director of Military Organisation, Joseph Plunkett, their Director of Military Operations, and Eamonn Ceannt, their Director of Communications. Soon afterwards they were joined by Tom Clarke and Sean MacDermott and, much later, by Thomas MacDonagh, the Volunteers' Director of Training.

The most significant member of this group was Patrick Pearse. Pearse had been the editor of the Gaelic League's newspaper, and already two themes had begun to appear in his writings and speeches which were to have a profound influence both on the rising itself and on the significance which was later given to it in the national mythology. One of these ideas can only be described as a Messianic complex – the belief that he was called upon to die for the people in order to redeem the nation – 'One man can free a people, as one Man redeemed the world'. Linked with this was the idea of blood sacrifice – that success did not necessarily mean military victory but rather that a number of men should be seen to have taken up arms and died for Ireland. 'The last sixth months have been the most glorious in the history of Europe' he wrote, late in 1915. 'It is good for the world that such things should be done. The old heart of the earth needed to be warmed with the red wine of the battlefields. Such august homage was never before offered to God as this, the homage of millions of lives gladly given for love of country.' This was more than an individual idiosyn-

cracy. Not only was the idea shared by several of his friends and colleagues – poets, Catholics, Gaelic enthusiasts and revolutionary romantics like himself – the idea also appears, for example, in one of Rupert Brooke's war poems.

Blow out, you bugles, over the rich Dead!
There's none of these so lonely and poor of old,
But, dying, has made us rarer gifts than gold.
These laid the world away; poured out the red
Sweet wine of youth; gave up the years to be
Of work and joy, and that unhoped serene
That men call age; and those who would have been,
Their sons, they gave their immortality.

Connolly reacted violently at first – 'No, we do not think the old heart of the earth needs to be warmed with the red wine of millions of lives. We think anyone who does is a blithering idiot' – but by 1916 even he had come round to believing something very similar – 'we recognise that of us, as of mankind before Calvary, it may truly be said – without the shedding of Blood there is no redemption'.

Connolly, in fact, had caused the secret group within the IRB some concern. They could not be sure that his belief in a socialist republic might not prove stronger than his belief in national independence, and that, if so, his small but effective Citizen Army might not rise in rebellion independently. Early in 1916 therefore Connolly was persuaded to co-operate with the IRB's Military Committee; he was to emerge as one of its most forceful members.

At about the same time MacNeill (who was aware of Pearse's ideas and disagreed fundamentally with them) became increasingly uneasy about what he suspected were plans for an armed rising. 'The only possible basis for successful revolutionary action is deep and widespread popular discontent' he wrote in February 1916. 'We have only to look around us in the streets to realise that no such condition exists in Ireland. I wish it to be clearly understood that under present conditions I am definitely opposed to any preparations that may come forward involving insurrec-

tion.' Although Pearse, MacDonagh and Plunkett all assured him that nothing of the kind was planned, the date for the insurrection had in fact already been fixed; it was, significantly, to be Easter Sunday, 23 April 1916.

The original plan had been for a nationwide rising, but this proved impracticable. Partly this was because of the secrecy with which the Military Committee operated – not only did most of the local Volunteer commanders know nothing about a rising, even the other members of the IRB Supreme Council were not told of the plans. The substitution of a Dublin rising for a nationwide insurrection was also due to the inability of Sir Roger Casement – who had spent most of the war there – to obtain any practical assistance from Germany. When finally the Germans agreed to send a shipload of arms, the ship was intercepted off the Kerry coast, and Casement (who had been landed in Ireland from a German submarine) was captured, tried and executed for treason.

By the time Casement was captured however, on Good Friday, 21 April 1916, plans for the rising were well advanced. Once again MacNeill had become suspicious – and once again Pearse had reassured him. It was not until Saturday, April 22nd that he finally learned the whole truth. That evening there was an angry confrontation between Pearse and MacNeill, in which Pearse said: 'We have used your name and influence for what they were worth, but we have done with you now. It is no use trying to stop us: our plans are all made and will be carried out'.

MacNeill at once cancelled the manoeuvres which Pearse had ordered for Easter Sunday as a cover for the rising. It was this – and the loss of the German arms – which finally decided that the national insurrection would be replaced by a local protest in arms. On the Sunday morning the Military Committee met and decided to start a rising in Dublin at 12 noon on Monday, 24 April with such forces as they could muster.[4] At first the 1,600 men who answered the call had the ad-

---

[4] In spite of MacNeill's orders there were a few isolated outbreaks outside the city, notably in county Dublin, but none achieved more than temporary success.

*The order signed by Eoin MacNeill on Saturday, 22 April 1916
cancelling the manoeuvres which Pearse had ordered for Easter Sunday,
23 April, as a cover for the Rising, and (bottom) the surrender order,
signed by Parnell, Connolly and MacDonagh a week later on Saturday
29 April.*

vantage of surprise and were able to seize a number of
key positions, including the GPO. It was here, at about
midday on Monday, 24 April, that Pearse read out a
proclamation declaring the establishment of an Irish
Republic.[5] 'The response was chilling' said an eye-
witness; 'a few, thin, perfunctory cheers, no direct
hostility just then, but no enthusiasm whatever.'

But although the Proclamation made little impact
on Easter Monday, it was to have a profound influence
in the future. By claiming that the rising was the latest
in a long line dedicated to the assertion of national
independence by force of arms the Proclamation an-
chored the Easter Rising firmly to the Irish revolutionary tradition. By declaring the establishment of a
Republic it created a point of departure for all those
who looked back to it as the justification for their
actions in the years to follow.

The insurgents soon lost their early advantage. Some
of the men with Eamon de Valera, the Volunteers'
commandant at Bolands Mill, ambushed a relief
column of British troops on Mount Street Bridge, and
inflicted heavy casualties, but it was an isolated success.
On Wednesday, the British army began shelling the
rebels' positions. On Friday they were forced to evacu-
ate the GPO. The next day Pearse surrendered and the
other commandants, isolated by now in various parts
of Dublin, followed him. The immediate reaction of
the vast majority of the population – especially in
Dublin – was very hostile. Not only had 450 people
been killed and 2,600 wounded – many of them civil-
ians – but £2½ million worth of damage had been done
and 100,000 people, a third of the city's population,
were on relief. Redmond probably judged rightly
when he declared in the House of Commons that his
feelings of detestation and horror were shared by 'the
overwhelming mass of the people of Ireland'. 'It is not
an *Irish* rebellion', wrote Augustine Birrell, the Chief
Secretary for Ireland, who now had to resign; 'it
would be a pity if ex post facto it became one and was
added to the long and melancholy list of Irish rebellions.'

[5] The full text is shown overleaf.

POBLACHT NA H EIREANN.

THE PROVISIONAL GOVERNMENT

OF THE

IRISH REPUBLIC

TO THE PEOPLE OF IRELAND.

IRISHMEN AND IRISHWOMEN: In the name of God and of the dead generations fro m which she receives her old tradition of nationhood, Ireland, through us, summons her children to her flag and strikes for her. freedom.

Having organised and trained her manhood through her secret revolutionary organisation, the Irish Republican Brotherhood, and through her open military organisations, the Irish Volunteers and the Irish Citizen Army, having patiently perfected her discipline, having resolutely waited for the right moment to reveal itself, she now seizes that moment, and, supported by her exiled children in America and by gallant allies in Europe, but relying in the first on her own strength, she strikes in full confidence of victory.

We declare the right of the people of Ireland to the ownership of Ireland, and to the unfettered control of Irish destinies, to be sovereign and indefeasible. The long usurpation of that right by a foreign people and government has not extinguished the right, nor can it ever be extinguished except by the destruction of the Irish people. In every generation the Irish people have asserted their right to national freedom and sovereignty; six times during the past three hundred years they have asserted it in arms. Standing on that fundamental right and again asserting it in arms in the face of the world, we hereby proclaim the Irish Republic as a Sovereign Independent State, and we pledge our lives and the lives of our comrades-in-arms to the cause of its freedom, of its welfare, and of its exaltation among the nations.

The Irish Republic is entitled to, and hereby claims, the allegiance of every Irishman and Irishwoman. The Republic guarantees religious and civil liberty, equal rights and equal opportunities to all its citizens, and declares its resolve to pursue the happiness and prosperity of the whole nation and of all its parts, cherishing all the children of the nation equally, and oblivious of the differences carefully fostered by an alien government, which have divided a minority from the majority in the past.

Until our arms have brought the opportune moment for the establishment of a permanent National Government, representative of the whole people of Ireland and elected by the suffrages of all her men and women, the Provisional Government, hereby constituted, will administer the civil and military affairs of the Republic in trust for the people.

We place the cause of the Irish Republic under the protection of the Most High God, Whose blessing we invoke upon our arms, and we pray that no one who serves that cause will dishonour it by cowardice, inhumanity, or rapine. In this supreme hour the Irish nation must, by its valour and discipline and by the readiness of its children to sacrifice themselves for the common good, prove itself worthy of the august destiny to which it is called.

Signed on Behalf of the Provisional Government,

THOMAS J. CLARKE,

SEAN Mac DIARMADA,   **THOMAS MacDONAGH,**

P. H. PEARSE,   **EAMONN CEANNT,**

JAMES CONNOLLY.   **JOSEPH PLUNKETT**

But that was exactly what happened. The execution of 14 of the leaders of the Dublin rising, spread out over ten days, turned public hostility to the rebels into anger and disgust with the British; one of the last to be shot was James Connolly, so ill from a gangrenous leg wound that he had to be strapped to a chair for sentence to be carried out. In the circumstances – Britain was after all in the middle of a war with Germany, and more than 150,000 Irishmen were fighting in the British army – some executions were probably inevitable. But, as Bernard Shaw wrote in the *Daily News*: 'It is absolutely impossible to slaughter a man in this position without making him a martyr and a hero'. Just how quickly this happened is shown by an incident related by the Nationalist MP, T. P. O'Connor: 'A little girl walking with her mother through the streets begged to be given a new hat. Her mother refused; then the child began praying to "St Pearse" to herself. In the end, after some words, the mother changed her mind and bought the child a hat.' John Dillon, one of the leading Nationalist MPs, who had been in Dublin throughout the rising, warned Redmond: 'It would really not be possible to exaggerate the desperate character of the situation here', and on May 11th in the House of Commons, he declared: 'You are letting loose a river of blood, and made no mistake about it, between two races who, after 300 years of hatred and strife, we had nearly succeeded in bringing together.'

This was only the beginning. Several thousand suspects were rounded up after the rising and nearly 2,000 of them were interned in British gaols. Many young men were swept into the net who had nothing to do either with the rising or with extremism, but who, by the time they were released, had become diehard republicans. And, though the crowds had jeered them as they left Dublin, they were greeted as heroes when they returned.

As the war had dragged on and the prospect of Home Rule receded the widespread support for the parliamentary party had begun to evaporate. This change in the public mood was now influenced by the failure of the Home Rule negotiations which Asquith re-opened soon after the rising. With great difficulty Redmond managed to persuade his party to accept the temporary exclusion – as he thought – of six Ulster counties. Carson however had extracted from Lloyd George – who was in charge of the negotiations – a written assurance that the exclusion would be permanent. 'We must make it clear', wrote Lloyd George, 'that at the end of the period Ulster does not, whether she wills it or not, merge in the rest of Ireland'. When, in July 1916, this assurance became public, the negotiations immediately broke down. 'The idea of our agreeing to the partition of our nation is unthinkable' said Redmond. The breakdown of the negotiations was a severe blow to the prestige and influence of the parliamentary party, for Home Rule now seemed impossible without partition and that, outside Ulster, was totally unacceptable.

But no coherent alternative organisation yet existed to articulate the new mood. The government, and the public at large, had called the Easter Rising a Sinn Fein rebellion. The Rising, of course, had nothing to do with Sinn Fein; the main question now indeed was whether moderates like Griffith and MacNeill could co-operate effectively with extreme republicans, either as Sinn Fein, or as anything else. During 1917, however, both wings worked together to defeat the Nationalists in three by-elections, ending in July with the spectacular victory of Eamon de Valera at East Clare. His victory was received with an enthusiasm 'unprecedented in the history of Irish political contests'. But though de Valera had declared that he stood for Irish independence, he never defined either the form that independence was to take, nor how it was to be achieved. At the Sinn Fein convention in October 1917, de Valera was elected president and the movement's aims redefined: 'Sinn Fein aims at securing the international recognition of Ireland as an independent Irish Republic. Having achieved that status, the Irish people may by referendum freely choose their own form of government'. This preserved a united front between moderates and republicans inside Sinn Fein, but the ambiguity – both about means and ends – remained.

But Home Rule seemed as far away as ever, and the breakdown (in March 1918) of an all-party Irish Convention, which had been set up to find a solution to the problem, further discredited the parliamentary party. And whilst the British government was unwilling to stir up public feeling by cracking down too hard on the republicans, it did enough – through intermittent persecution – to ensure that Sinn Fein continued to attract support.

And then, in April 1918, public opinion was outraged by the decision to apply conscription to Ireland, and to offer Home Rule immediately for 26 counties in exchange. The Nationalist party withdrew from Westminster in protest. After a conference in Dublin between representatives of the party, Sinn Fein and the trades unions, a declaration was issued denouncing the attempt to enforce conscription as an 'unwarrantable aggression which we call upon all true Irishmen to resist by the most effective means at their disposal', and the Catholic hierarchy denounced it as 'an oppressive and inhuman law, which the Irish have a right to resist by every means that are consonant with the laws of God'.

To many it seemed the final proof that constitutional methods had failed and it was not surprising that, in the election of December 1918, Sinn Fein won 73 of the 105 Irish seats; the Nationalists were reduced to 6. Redmond, who had died in March, was spared this final humiliation, but Dillon, who had succeeded him, was decisively beaten by de Valera in East Mayo.

With this victory Sinn Fein was transformed overnight from an outlawed organisation into a potential government. Its aims, as set out in the party's election manifesto, were to ignore Westminster and set up a separate parliament in Ireland; to make use of 'any and every means' to get rid of British rule in Ireland; and to appeal to the Peace Conference at Versailles for the establishment of Ireland as a separate nation. The appeal to the Peace Conference fell on deaf ears, but in January 1919 the 27 Sinn Fein MP's who were not in prison met and established themselves as Dail Eireann – the parliament of the Irish Republic. They declared that 'the Irish Republic was proclaimed in Dublin on Easter Monday 1916' and ratified its existence, appointed a provisional government, and set about establishing an alternative administration which would ignore the British (in which, especially after the local elections in 1920, they were remarkably successful). In April, a second Dail met and appointed a government with de Valera as President.

With two rival governments in existence a clash was inevitable. Indeed on the day the first Dail had met, the first shots were fired in what was soon to become the Anglo-Irish war. Though de Valera was also President of the Volunteers, and though the Dail had formally asserted its authority over them, the Volunteers (now the Irish Republican Army) acted largely on their own authority. For, just as the IRB had previously infiltrated the Irish Volunteers, now under a new leader, Michael Collins, they were equally quick to take over the IRA. Collins was quite clear about his strategy: 'the sooner fighting is forced and a general state of disorder created through the country', he is reported to have said, 'the better it will be for the country'.

The war that followed, like all wars of this kind, began nastily and got nastier still as it went on. Beginning with raids and ambushes, it developed first into a campaign of reprisals and counter-reprisals, and finally into full-scale guerilla warfare. The IRA's aim was to make normal government impossible and the cost of holding the country down too great. On the British side, the war was fought largely by the army, and later by two forces of special armed police – the Black and Tans and the Auxiliaries as well. Faced with an enemy who could not easily be identified, and with an increasingly hostile population, they reacted by taking unauthorised reprisals – as at Balbriggan in Co. Dublin – in areas where they had been attacked. Terrible things were done on both sides. On 12 November 1920 in Dublin – Bloody Sunday – the IRA assassinated 14 British military intelligence officers in the morning, some in front of their wives and children; the same afternoon Black and Tans, who claimed to have been fired on first, opened fire on the crowd at a Gaelic foot-ball match at Croke Park, killing 12 and wounding 60.

In Britain the struggle was viewed with a distaste which rapidly hardened into disgust. 'An army already perilously undisciplined, and a police force avowedly beyond control, have defiled, by heinous acts, the reputation of England', thundered *The Times*, and in the House of Lords the Archbishop of Canterbury declared that 'the undisciplined forces of the Crown, appointed to suppress disorder, have themselves, though without definite superior authority and command, given terrible examples of the very kind of disorder which they are sent there to suppress'.

In December 1919 Lloyd George announced his latest attempt at a solution – the Government of Ireland Bill, which passed into law during 1920. It was accompanied – as such measures had so often been accompanied in the past – by further attempts at coercion. The Act established two Home Rule parliaments in Ireland, one in Belfast for the six north-eastern counties – Northern Ireland – and another in Dublin for the remaining twenty-six counties – Southern Ireland.[6]

Elections were held in May 1921, and Sinn Fein, treating the elections as those for the third Dail, was returned unopposed in 124 of the 128 seats in Southern Ireland (4 Independents were returned for Dublin University). A few days later, in a spectacular gesture of defiance, the IRA attacked and burnt down the Custom House in Dublin – effectively the headquarters of the British civil administration in Ireland. After two years the British government had to face the choice either of systematic conquest, or of offering terms which Sinn Fein would accept. But the IRA could not win either; it had succeeded in making normal government impossible, and it had established its own administration in many parts of the country, but it could not force the British to withdraw. And though survivors disagree, it seems likely that by the middle of 1921 the IRA were running dangerously short of arms and ammunition.

Several attempts at opening peace negotiations had been made since the previous autumn, but it proved extraordinarily difficult to bring the two sides to the conference table. De Valera continued to insist on an all-Ireland republic. Lloyd George, on the other hand, though he was beginning to accept the necessity for a larger degree of self-government, regarded a Republic as out of the question, and was not prepared to coerce Ulster, which now – under the Government of Ireland Act – had its own parliament.

Eventually, in May 1921, a new opportunity came when King George V went to Belfast to open Northern Ireland's first parliament. 'I speak from a full heart', he said, 'when I pray that my coming to Ireland today may prove to be the first step towards the end of strife amongst her people, whatever their race or creed. In that hope I appeal to all Irishmen to pause, to stretch out the hand of forbearance and conciliation, to forgive and forget, and to join in making for the land they love a new era of peace, contentment and goodwill.'

The King's appeal helped to create a favourable climate for negotiations in Britain, and when Lloyd George offered de Valera talks on much more favourable terms than before, de Valera – influenced no doubt by the critical position of the IRA – accepted. On 11 July 1921 accordingly, a truce was declared. At midnight the violence, which had continued almost until the last moment, suddenly stopped, and its place was taken by an uneasy peace.

Perhaps a few words of explanation are needed about the chapter title: Green, white and gold. *The flag of the Irish Republic is in fact green, white and* orange. *The fact that Nationalist enthusiasm has changed the orange to gold is, say Unionists, only natural; gold, after all, is the papal colour.*

[6] For events in the North during this period see chapter 7 (pp. 92–101).

Left: Sackville Street (now O'Connell Street) Dublin towards the end of the Easter Rising, showing the fires out of control on the eastern side of the street, with the Parnell and Nelson monuments clearly outlined against the flames, and (below) after the Rising, from the ruins of these burned-out buildings, with the shell of the GPO in the background.

Right: Pearse, on the right, surrenders to Brigadier General W H M Lowe on the pavement at the corner of Moore Street and Parnell Street, at 2.30pm on Saturday, 29 April 1916.

Below: de Valera, beneath the white cross, at the head of the men with whom he had held Bolands Mill, being marched away under armed guard after the surrender – 'Fine looking fellows', recorded an onlooker, 'swinging along in good step'.

Left: a British soldier points to the spot in the yard at Kilmainham gaol, Dublin, where fourteen of the leaders of the Easter Rising were executed.

Below: the crowds who turned out in Dublin to welcome the last 117 of nearly 2000 men detained after the Rising and released in June 1917.

One of those released was Eamon de Valera, chosen as the Sinn Fein candidate for a bye-election in East Clare in July 1917. He heard the result dressed in his Volunteer uniform (right) declaring that this crushing victory over the Nationalist candidate was a 'monument to those glorious men' who had died in 1916. In May 1918 de Valera shared an anti-conscription platform with John Dillon, the leader of the Nationalist party, in Dillon's home town, Ballaghadereen, Co Roscommon (below right). In the election of December 1918 de Valera defeated Dillon in the seat at East Mayo which he had held since 1885.

Page 82, top: a Sinn Fein district court at Westport, Co Mayo – one of the hierarchy of 'Dail Courts' established in June 1920 to replace the British machinery of justice. Though they were declared illegal, nearly a thousand of these courts survived until the truce in July 1921.

Page 82, bottom: the meeting of the second Dail in the Mansion House, Dublin, in August 1921 – the first to be held in public – which rejected Lloyd George's first offer of peace terms to de Valera.

FREEDOM TO ACHIEVE FREEDOM

'For five terrible years', wrote a Republican pamphleteer after the truce in 1921, 'the nation had remained united on three great principles:

1 The existence of the Republic founded in Easter Week, and confirmed by national plebiscite in 1918;
2 The sanctity of our national independence declared by the Sovereign National Assembly in January 1919; and
3 The territorial integrity of Ireland, which had outlasted history itself'.

For the last fifty years Irish political life has been haunted by the insistence of an intransigent minority that they alone are faithful to these principles, and by their determination to uphold them 'with the threat of, if not the actual use of, physical force'. The majority on the other hand have taken the view that, whilst these principles were important, they were not so fundamental that they demanded the rejection of any alternative, especially when this alternative offered the country a significant measure of independence. This basic disagreement goes back to the negotiations for the treaty which set up the Irish Free State in December 1921.

It was in fact several months after the truce was declared in June 1921 before real negotiations started. First there was a protracted correspondence between de Valera and Lloyd George in which de Valera tried to get Lloyd George to accept him as the President of an Irish Republic, and Lloyd George steadfastly refused to acknowledge that Ireland could unilaterally renounce her allegiance to the crown and her membership of the British Empire. De Valera then formulated his idea of External Association – that is, a connection between Ireland and the Empire for certain common purposes, provided that Ireland – all Ireland – functioned *internally* as a Republic: 'A certain treaty of free association with the British Commonwealth group, as with a partial league of nations, we would have been ready to contemplate, and as a government to negotiate and take responsibility for', he wrote, 'had we an assurance that the entry of the nation as a whole into such association would secure for it the allegiance of the present dissenting minority [meaning Northern Ireland] to meet whose sentiments alone this step could be contemplated'. Once again, Lloyd George replied that no British government could 'acknowledge the right of Ireland to secede from her allegiance to the king'.[1]

Finally, at the end of September, Lloyd George invited the Irish to a conference in London on October 11th 'where we can meet your delegates as spokesmen of the people whom you represent, with a view to ascertaining how the association of Ireland with the community of nations known as the British Empire may be reconciled with Irish national aspirations', and De Valera, finding this ingenious formula acceptable, replied: 'We agree that conference, not correspondence, is the most practical and hopeful way to an understanding. We accept the invitation'.

The Irish delegation was led by Arthur Griffith and Michael Collins. But de Valera, and the more intransigent republicans in the Cabinet, stayed at home. This potential source of friction was increased by the fact that the delegation's status was far from clear. Their credentials described them as 'envoys plenipotentiary from the elected Government of the Republic of Ireland to negotiate and conclude with the representatives of His Britannic Majesty George V a Treaty or Treaties of association and accommodation between Ireland and the Community of Nations known as the British Commonwealth' – which seemed to mean that they had the power to negotiate and sign a Treaty. But before they left Dublin the delegates received final instructions which included the clause: 'It is also understood that the complete text of the draft treaty about to be signed will be similarly submitted to Dublin and reply awaited'.

The negotiations were largely concerned with defining, in a way that both sides could accept, the exact status of the new Irish State. This explains why so much

[1] Ironically enough, though it was unacceptable in 1921, this principle was recognised only ten years later in the Statute of Westminster (which established a new constitutional relationship between the United Kingdom and its overseas Dominions) and it was precisely on such terms that India was to remain in the Commonwealth when she became a Republic in 1948.

time was taken up in arguing about the oath of allegiance which was to be written into its constitution. For de Valera and the republicans, *any* oath of allegiance was a betrayal of the oath they had all taken to the Republic. 'We are all here at one', he wrote to Griffith, 'that there can be no question of our asking the Irish people to enter an arrangement which could make them subject to the Crown, or demand from them allegiance to the British King.' To their delegates on the spot, however, who could not see how, if the British refused to compromise on the issue, they could prevent such an arrangement, an oath of allegiance seemed a tolerable price to pay for the large amount of self-government which Britain was prepared to concede in return. And the final version of the oath was indeed considerably modified to meet Irish susceptibilities, though it still contained an undertaking to 'be faithful to HM King George V, his heirs and successors'.

Though the Irish delegation was prepared to compromise over the oath, they were determined to insist on the essential unity of Ireland. It might have been expected therefore that the question of Ulster would have been crucial, and Griffith's instructions were certainly that if he had to break off the negotiations this should be over Ulster. But there was already a parliament and a government in existence in Northern Ireland, whose Prime Minister Sir James Craig simply refused to accept an all-Ireland parliament.[2] And though Lloyd George put pressure on Craig he could not in the end coerce him, not least because Lloyd George was the Prime Minister of a coalition government which contained many powerful and influential Unionists.

And there was another and more significant reason why the negotiations did not break down. Lloyd George persuaded first Griffith, and then the other members of the Irish delegation, to agree to a Boundary Commission. What this meant was that if Northern Ireland refused to accept an all-Ireland parliament, then the frontier would be revised by a Boundary Commission 'which would be directed to adjust the line by inclusion and exclusion so as to make the boundary conform as closely as possible to the wishes of the people'. This persuaded the Irish delegation that the Commission would award such substantial areas of the six counties to the Free State that Northern Ireland would no longer be viable. As Collins calculated: 'We would save Tyrone and Fermanagh, parts of Derry, Armagh and Down by the Boundary Commission'.

Finally, on the evening of 5 December, Lloyd George insisted that the delegates 'must sign the Treaty or else quit'. Holding up two letters, he said that he must communicate with Sir James Craig that night. 'Here are the alternative letters which I have prepared, one enclosing Articles of Agreement reached by His Majesty's Government and yourselves, and the other saying that the Sinn Fein representatives refuse to come within the Empire. If I send this letter it is war, and war within three days. Which letter am I to send?'

At ten to three the following morning, 6 December 1921, the Irish delegation signed the Articles of Agreement for the Treaty which created the Irish Free State. The Irish had gained a greater measure of independence than they had ever achieved before, but they had not achieved either a Republic or External Association. Lloyd George, on the other hand, had realised both his original aims: the Free State would remain within the Empire, and Northern Ireland would not be coerced into inclusion.

The Irish Cabinet was split in two. After a grim debate lasting several hours, its members voted 4-3 to accept the Treaty. De Valera at once issued a statement to the press: 'The terms of this Agreement are in violent conflict with the wishes of the majority of the nation as expressed freely in successive elections during the past three years. I feel it my duty to inform you immediately that I cannot recommend the acceptance of this Treaty'. Griffith replied: 'I believe that this Treaty will lay the foundation of peace and friendship between the two nations. What I have signed I

[2] For the events of this period in Northern Ireland, see chapter 7 (pp. 92–101).

will stand by, in the belief that the end of the conflict of centuries is at hand'.

This division within the Cabinet was mirrored in the Dail, which met on 14 December for the first of the thirteen sessions in which the Treaty was debated, and which, as time went on, became increasingly rancorous and abusive. Griffith opened the debate. 'We have brought back to Ireland her full rights and powers of fiscal control' he declared. 'We have brought back to Ireland equality with England, equality with all nations which form that Commonwealth, and an equal voice in the direction of foreign affairs in peace and war'. He admitted that 'we took an oath to the Irish Republic, but, as President de Valera himself said, he understood that oath to bind him to do the best he could for Ireland. So do we. We have done the best we could for Ireland'. It was not good enough for President de Valera. 'I am against this Treaty because it does not reconcile Irish national aspirations with association with the British Government . . . it gives away Irish independence; it acknowledges the head of the British Empire not merely as the head of an association, but as the direct monarch of Ireland'. Collins returned to the defence: 'I say if we all stood on the recognition of the Irish Republic as a prelude to any conference, we could very easily have said so and there would be no conference'. The Treaty did not give them recognition of the Irish Republic, but it gave them freedom – 'not the ultimate freedom that all nations aspire and develop to, but the freedom to achieve it'. Another supporter of the Treaty, Kevin O'Higgins, put the point even more bluntly: 'It represents such a broad measure of liberty for the Irish people and it acknowledges such a large proportion of its rights, you are not entitled to reject it without being able to show them you have a reasonable prospect of achieving more'.

De Valera still believed that he could. On 4 January he circulated his Document No 2 as an alternative to the Treaty. Its main clauses provided, first, 'that the legislative, executive and judicial authority of Ireland shall be derived from the people of Ireland';

second, 'that, for the purposes of common concern, Ireland shall be associated with the states of the British Commonwealth'; and finally, 'that for the purposes of the Association, Ireland shall recognise His Britannic Majesty as head of the Association'. This formula, De Valera argued, could be reconciled both with the oath they had all sworn to the Irish Republic, and to the demands of the British government. Even if this were true, however, it was too late to prevent a fundamental break. On 7 January 1922 the Dail divided. 64 members voted in favour of the Treaty, 57 against.

Such a narrow margin meant that the defeated side was unlikely to accept the verdict, and of course it did not. De Valera resigned, the pro-Treaty members of the Dail elected Griffith President in his place, and Collins was appointed head of the Provisional Government which would take over from the British authorities. In March de Valera made a series of speeches which sounded an ominous warning to his supporters. If they wanted to complete their work, he said, 'they would have to complete it, not over the bodies of foreign soldiers, but over the dead bodies of their own countrymen. They would have to wade through Irish blood, through the blood of the soldiers of the Irish Government and through, perhaps, the blood of some of the members of the Government in order to get Irish freedom'.

What was probably even more important was that there was a split within the IRA. Republicans in the army held a convention on 26 March in which they reaffirmed the army's allegiance to the Republic, repudiated the authority of the Dail and set up their own executive. 'We have declared for an Irish Republic', said Liam Lynch, 'and we will not live under any other law'. On 14 April some of these 'Irregulars' seized the Four Courts and other buildings in Dublin. Outside Dublin there were a growing number of incidents between pro- and anti-Treaty groups within the Free State army, as both took over from the evacuating British.

The Provisional Government was now in a difficult position. If they attacked the Irregulars they might start a civil war; if they did not attack them, they might themselves be overthrown. Collins tried to compromise with an Army Document – signed by both pro- and anti-Treaty representatives in the army – which called for an 'agreed election' and the formation of a government which had the whole country's support. But the Provisional Government had also to produce a Constitution for the new State. If de Valera thought that it was insufficiently Republican he would oppose it; if, on the other hand, he found it acceptable, the British government would be certain to reject it. Once again, Collins tried to compromise. He arranged with de Valera to fight the Election for the new Dail so that it would produce a coalition 'without prejudice to their present respective positions'.

The election – which was effectively (though not in Republican eyes) a popular referendum on the Treaty – produced 58 government supporters in favour, and 38 against the Treaty, but 32 independents were also elected and polled more votes than either; and most of these independents also supported the Treaty. The result was declared on 24 June. Two days earlier however Sir Henry Wilson, Northern Ireland's military adviser, had been assassinated in London by two IRA men. On 26 June the British government denounced the murder and hinted strongly that unless the Provisional Government was prepared to move against the Irregulars, it would 'resume full liberty of action in any direction that may seem proper'. On the same day General O'Connell, Collins' Deputy Chief of Staff, was kidnapped by the Irregulars in the Four Courts. Collins at once ordered them to surrender; they refused, and on 30 June, with field guns borrowed from the departing British, the Irregulars were shelled into submission.

The attack on the Four Courts was a signal for the outbreak of general warfare between pro-Treaty and anti-Treaty forces throughout the country. The war began with a series of set-piece engagements. At the end of July the Free State army took Limerick and Waterford; a few weeks later, on 12 August, they entered Cork. The war then degenerated into a pro-tracted, straggling and bitter guerilla campaign. Though Griffith died and Collins was killed in an ambush at the end of August, their successors, W. T. Cosgrave (as head of the government) and Richard Mulcahy (as commander-in-chief) were equally determined to win. The second Dail was never dissolved, and refusing – with his supporters – to acknowledge the authority of the new Dail elected in June 1922, de Valera set up a Republican government in October; but though he claimed the authority, he had in fact little control over the Irregulars, who could not count on the solid support of the civilian population either. The weight of their authority and military power slowly tilted the scales in the government's favour, and as they began to gain the upper hand, the war degenerated into a series of attacks and reprisals.

In December a member of the Dail was murdered, and the next day four Republican prisoners were shot. 73 more Republicans were to be executed by the government in similar reprisals before the end of the war. Many terrible things were done on both sides, far worse in many cases than in the war against the British. As a result, what had begun as a high-toned difference of principle ended as an irreconcilable blood feud that was to poison Irish political life for years. Finally, in May 1923, their Chief of Staff, Frank Aiken, agreed with de Valera that the Irregulars would have to negotiate a truce. On 24 May de Valera called on the Irregulars to lay down – though not to surrender – their arms. 'Soldiers of the Republic, Legion of the Rearguard', ran his message, 'The Republic can no longer be defended successfully by your arms. Further sacrifice of life would now be vain and continuance of the struggle in arms unwise in the national interest and prejudicial to the future of our cause. Military victory must be allowed to rest for the moment with those who have destroyed the Republic'.

Both the extent and the limitations of that victory were indicated by the result of the general election held in August 1923. Cumann na nGaedheal, the party formed by supporters of the Treaty, and led by W. T. Cosgrave, won 63 seats. Though the Sinn Fein party, led by de Valera, won 44 seats, they refused to sit in the Dail because this would have meant taking 'an oath of allegiance to a foreign King'. But abstention from the Dail meant that the party now became the impotent spectator of a government which managed to govern very effectively without them. In March 1926, at the Sinn Fein annual convention, de Valera proposed that, if the oath were abolished, attendance at the Dail should become 'a question not of principle, but of policy'. The motion was narrowly defeated, and in May, de Valera resigned from Sinn Fein and launched a new party, Fianna Fail. He was followed by many of his supporters, and at the election of June 1927, Fianna Fail won 44 seats; but his party still refused to take the oath of allegiance.

In July however, Kevin O'Higgins, Cosgrave's able and outspoken Minister of Home Affairs, was assassinated. The government immediately introduced an Electoral Amendment Bill which provided that all candidates in elections must undertake, when nominated, to take the oath of allegiance. Two of de Valera's supporters had in fact already taken the oath, and on 10 August 1927, de Valera and the remaining 41 members of Fianna Fail entered the Dail. They issued a document which claimed that the oath was not an oath, but 'merely an empty political formula which Deputies could conscientiously sign without becoming involved, or without involving their nation, in obligations of loyalty to the English crown'. De Valera underlined the position. 'I want you to understand', he said to the Clerk, 'that I am not taking any oath nor giving any promise of faithfulness to the King of England or to any power outside the people of Ireland. I am putting my name here merely as a formality to get the permission necessary to enter amongst the other Teachtai [deputies] that were elected by the people of Ireland, and I want you to know that no other meaning is to be attached to what I am doing.'

Once Fianna Fail had entered the Dail many people who sympathised with de Valera's position, but who had withheld their support whilst his party had excluded itself from normal political life, were once more prepared to vote for him. Fianna Fail also benefited from the pre-Keynesian solutions proposed by the Cosgrave government for the economic crisis of the early 1930s, and from the widespread support for its own populist programme which favoured the small farmer and the small business. And, though the party was careful to play down the connection, Fianna Fail received the valuable (and not always strictly democratic) support of the militant republicans in Sinn Fein and the IRA, who had remained outside Fianna Fail since 1926.

In the 1932 election Fianna Fail won 72 seats and de Valera formed his first government, and the next year, in another election, he won an overall majority in the Dail. It was a remarkable victory, both for constitutional methods and for responsible parliamentary opposition. Cumann na nGaedheal had forced Fianna Fail into the Dail, and had accepted their consequent electoral defeat. Fianna Fail, in spite of the claim of one deputy that they were only a 'slightly constitutional party' had disowned their more militant supporters and proved that they were prepared to work the system.

For thirty-five of the next forty-one years, Fianna Fail was in power, and for twenty-one of those thirty-five years, de Valera was prime minister.[3] Throughout this period the major opposition party was Fine Gael, founded in 1933 as the successor to Cumann na nGaedheal. The two main parties in the Irish Republic today therefore grew up around the two sides in the Civil War – Cumann na nGaedheal, and its successor Fine Gael, was the party of those who had supported the Treaty; Fianna Fail was the party of those who had opposed it. Forty years later that remains the major difference between them.

But it is not the only one. Though this has begun to change, especially since the mid-1960s, Fine Gael has tended to be more of a middle-class, middle-aged party. Moreover, once Fianna Fail had established itself as a responsible, non-revolutionary alter-

[3] The official title was President of the Legislative Council before the 1937 constitution, and Taoiseach afterwards.

native in 1932, many of the more prosperous farmers and businessmen (who had supported Cumann na nGaedheal during the early years of the Free State) transferred their allegiance to Fianna Fail; and the connection between Fianna Fail and the business community became increasingly marked during the 1960s. De Valera's leadership, the efficiency of the party machine and the skilful use of patronage all helped to ensure that Fianna Fail became increasingly regarded as the natural governing party; and the party's ability to adapt itself to changing conditions ensured its continuing electoral success in the 1960s. Fine Gael, on the other hand, though it was the senior partner in two coalition governments between 1948 and 1951, and between 1954 and 1957, has seemed unable until recently to establish itself as a convincing alternative.[4]

Perhaps the most curious feature of the Irish political scene to an English observer however is the position of the Labour party, which has yet to establish itself as a major party. In the early years of the Free State this was largely because politics was dominated by constitutional issues (and Labour had acknowledged this by withdrawing all its candidates in the 1918 election). Once Fianna Fail achieved power therefore, it attracted much of the radical, republican support that might otherwise have gone to Labour. Uninspiring leadership, internecine party quarrels and ecclesiastical disapproval of 'socialism' have all since helped to hold Labour back. Just as significant has been the fact that until very recently the party's support has been largely in rural areas; though this has begun to change in the last ten years, Labour still won only 7 of the 38 seats in the Greater Dublin area in the 1973 election.

The Treaty and the Civil War have therefore continued to have some influence on Irish political life. But, more important than that, they left behind them three items of unfinished business – the question of the country's constitutional status, the continuation of partition, and the survival of the IRA.

Though they had accepted the Treaty because they believed it was the best settlement they could get at the time, its supporters were far from satisfied with it as a permanent arrangement. They had to prove, both to their own supporters and to their opponents, that the Treaty did indeed give them, as Collins had said, the freedom to achieve freedom. It is not surprising therefore that the Irish, with the active collaboration and support of Canada and South Africa, should have played a leading part during the 1920s in the series of Imperial Conferences that led to the de facto assertion of the independence of Commonwealth countries which was acknowledged in the Statute of Westminster in 1931. Five years before Arthur Balfour had defined their new position as 'autonomous communities within the British Empire, equal in status, in no way subordinate one to another in any aspect of their domestic or external affairs, though united by a common allegiance to the Crown and freely associated as members of the British Commonwealth of Nations'.

It was inevitable that, when de Valera came to power, the speed of the dismantling process should have been sharply increased. Since he had decided that there was no future in doctrinaire republicanism, he was bound, by the same logic as the Cosgrave government, to show that more could be achieved by diplomatic pressure than by violence. But de Valera was also dedicated to his own idea of External Association, and between 1932 and 1939 his policy was directed entirely at substituting External Association for the status conferred on the Irish Free State by the Treaty in 1921. One of his first actions in office was to remove the oath of allegiance from the constitution. 'The Oath', said de Valera, 'is an intolerable burden to the people of this state and they have declared in the most formal manner that they desire its removal'; in May 1933 the oath was abolished. In December 1936, taking advantage of the confusion created by the Abdication crisis in England, de Valera introduced an External Relations Bill, which removed all direct references in the

[4] It is probably too early to say whether the formation of a third coalition government after the 1973 election will lead to any fundamental change in this situation.

Constitution both to the British crown and to its representative in Ireland, the Governor General. Since however, as a member of the Commonwealth, Ireland had to recognise the King as its head, the Bill also declared that 'the King so recognised may, and is hereby authorised to, act on behalf of Saorstat Eireann [the Irish Free State] . . . as and when advised by the Executive Council to do so'. In December 1937 de Valera introduced a new Constitution, which declared that Eire, or Ireland, was a 'sovereign, independent, democratic state' and made no reference either to the crown or the British Commonwealth. Though it claimed that 'the national territory consists of the whole island of Ireland' it did not establish an Irish Republic. To have given this name to a 26 county state when he had sworn allegiance to a 32 county Republic would for de Valera have been to betray the men of 1916.[5]

Finally, on Easter Monday 1949, Ireland did become a Republic. It may seem surprising that the Irish Republic should have been inaugurated not by Fianna Fail, but by the first inter-party coalition led by Fine Gael. This was partly because of the electoral success of one of their coalition partners, the Republican Clann na Poblachta, and partly a political move to steal Fianna Fail's clothes. But the main reason was undoubtedly that the prime minister, J. A. Costello, believed that to declare Ireland a Republic would finally take the gun out of Irish politics. In this belief he was however mistaken. Furthermore, neither the declaration of the Republic, nor the promulgation of the 1937 constitution did anything to reconcile Northern Ireland to the prospect of Irish unity. The British government's reaction however was remarkably phlegmatic, and the most striking result was that relations between the two countries continued to improve.

The remaining complication in this relationship was of course the continuation of partition. Griffith and Collins had accepted the Treaty in the belief that the Boundary Commission to be set up under the Treaty would award such substantial areas of Northern Ireland to the Free State that Northern Ireland would be unable to survive. But Northern Ireland refused to appoint a representative to the Commission and in 1924 therefore the British government appointed J. R. Fisher, a prominent Unionist. The Free State appointed Eoin MacNeill, and the neutral chairman was a South African, Mr Justice Feetham. The actual wording of Article XII of the Treaty charged the Commission to 'determine in accordance with the wishes of the inhabitants, *so far as may be compatible with economic and geographic conditions*, the boundaries between Northern Ireland and the Free State'. These words proved to be crucial, since Mr Justice Feetham interpreted them to mean that there should be no substantial alterations to the existing boundary. The terms of the Commission's report were apparently leaked to the *Morning Post* in London, which on 7 November 1925 reported that there would in fact be only minor changes in the boundary, and that some of these would actually favour the North. To forestall the violent reaction that might so easily have followed if these proposals had actually been implemented, the Cosgrave government signed an agreement, on 3 December 1925, with the two governments of Great Britain and Northern Ireland by which the boundary was to remain unchanged.

Even if the Boundary Commission *had* acted as Griffith and Collins had been led to expect, it is very difficult to see either why the Northern Ireland government should have accepted it, or how the British government could have enforced the recommendations. But though this Tripartite Agreement gave partition an element of permanence which it had not had before, it was not accepted in the south as a final settlement of the boundary issue at the time, and it is still not recognised as such today. In the words of the statement made by the all-party Anti-Partition Conference held in Dublin in January 1949: 'The essence of democracy lies in the right of a people freely to determine how they are to be governed. The unit for this self-determination is the nation. Ireland through a nationhood never questioned in almost 2,000 years has

[5] For the consequences in Northern Ireland see chapter 7 (pp. 92–101).

89

The changes in the boundary between Northern Ireland and the Irish Free State. Left, as disclosed by the Morning Post *on 7 November 1925 and right, as actually proposed by the Boundary Commission in its report, suppressed in 1925 and not published until 1969.*

——————— PRESENT BOUNDARY

- - - - - - - - PROBABLE CHANGES

················ DOUBTFUL CHANGE

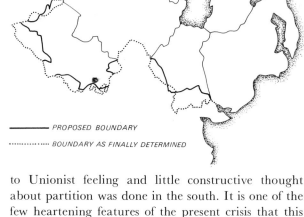

——————— PROPOSED BOUNDARY

················ BOUNDARY AS FINALLY DETERMINED

that right. Partition is the denial of the right to self-determination. . . . It was imposed by the British Government against the passionate protest of the overwhelming majority of the Irish people'; and the Conference therefore called upon the British Government and people: 'to end the present occupation of our Six North-Eastern counties and thereby enable the unity of Ireland to be restored and the age-long differences between the two nations brought to an end'.

Though the reunification of the national territory remained part of the stock in trade of politicians of all parties in the South for the next 40 years, it is difficult to avoid the suspicion that the louder they shouted the the less business they intended. Most of those who talked incessantly about ending partition knew perfectly well that the South was in no condition to take on the added burden of the Northern economy[6]. Furthermore these same politicians who preached the one-ness of Ireland were committed to the establishment of a state whose Gaelic and Catholic features were bound to be objectionable to Northern Protestants.[7] For 40 years after the Treaty no concession was made

to Unionist feeling and little constructive thought about partition was done in the south. It is one of the few heartening features of the present crisis that this total failure to come to terms with reality has at last been widely recognised.

For some however the issue remains a simple one. Even after de Valera came to power there remained a a group of irreconcilables. They believed, like de Valera, that a 32 county Republic has existed since Easter Monday 1916, and they were dedicated, like him, to making it a reality. Unlike de Valera, however, the IRA were not prepared to lay down their arms, 'for they still believe that the final changing of power will come only with the threat of, if not the actual use of, physical force'.

Though they have been continually haunted by the IRA's claim to be the only true heirs of Ireland's revolutionary heroes, Fianna Fail were prepared, once they were in power, to take quite exceptional measures to

[6] For the economic development of both parts of Ireland see chapter 8 (pp. 102–109).

[7] For these features see chapters 9 (pp. 114–121) and 10 (pp. 122–129).

deal with the extremists. In 1936 de Valera banned the IRA, and during the second world war a large number of its members were interned for the duration to safeguard Irish neutrality. The IRA has also suffered from its own internal divisions, and especially from continual arguments about whether the movement should be simply nationalist, or whether it should be Marxist as well.

Whether it was because of their internal feuds, or because of their quite remarkable incompetence, the actual impact of the IRA upon events was minimal. The bombing campaign in England in 1939 ended in complete failure. Nor were their efforts to co-operate with German agents during the war any more sucessful. As one of these agents remarked in exasperation: 'You know how to die for Ireland, but how to fight for her you have not the slightest idea'. The same inadequacy characterised the so-called 'border campaign' in 1957-62, at the end of which the IRA was left in complete disarray.

But the movement has always had just enough vitality, just enough continuity, to keep the old, simple, revolutionary tradition alive. Although the IRA was a perpetual skeleton at the feast, it was always possible, until recently to believe that it would gradually fade away. Now it is no longer possible to be so sure.

WHAT WE HAVE WE HOLD

'They had yelled about "No Home Rule" for a generation and then they were compelled to take a form of Home Rule that the Devil himself could never have imagined.' It was indeed ironic, as the Rev. J. B. Armour (almost a lone voice amongst Protestant churchmen in his support of Home Rule) said, that having resisted Home Rule for so long, Ulster Unionists should have been obliged, by the Government of Ireland Act of 1920, to accept a form of Home Rule for Northern Ireland. It is perhaps even more ironic that the Unionists' preferred alternative – direct rule from Westminster – should have been so bitterly attacked in the North when it was imposed by the Westminster government in March 1972. The strength of that reaction was an indication of the profound effect that the settlement of 1920 was to have on the subsequent development of Northern Ireland.

Even during the debates on the third Home Rule Bill, some members of the Liberal government had been prepared to consider the possibility of Ulster's being temporarily excluded from the Bill's operation. It proved impossible however to get both Unionists and Nationalists to agree – even at the Buckingham Palace Conference in 1914 – either on what parts of Ulster should be excluded, or if so, for how long this should be. At this stage the Unionists were convinced, in Carson's words, that 'If Ulster succeeds, Home Rule is dead', and their main objective was still to preserve the Union. In September 1914 however, the Home Rule Bill became law – although its operation was suspended until after the war, and although it was to be subject to an amending Bill which would deal with the position of Ulster.

When therefore, in the aftermath of the Easter Rising, Lloyd George revived the idea of excluding the six north-eastern counties from the operation of a Home Rule Bill as part of his proposed settlement, 'All I could do,' wrote Carson to Bonar Law, 'was to try and save something out of the wreckage'. In June 1916, therefore, he persuaded the Ulster Unionist Council to accept the principle of exclusion. 'We reaffirm our unabated abhorrence of the policy of Home Rule', they

resolved, but 'we feel, as loyal citizens, that, in this crisis of the Empire's history, it is our duty to make sacrifices'. As one of the Council's members, H. de F. Montgomery, wrote to his son: 'We could not possibly hope to get more than we were now offered without fighting. . . . If we did not agree to do this we should lose any remaining sympathy we had in Great Britain' and 'if we did not take this offer we should never get as good a one again'.

For much the same reason the Ulster Unionist Council agreed, in February 1920, to accept the establishment of the separate Parliament for the six north-eastern counties of Northern Ireland proposed in the Government of Ireland Act 'as the only means whereby the close connection of Ulster with Great Britain under the Act of Union could at that time be preserved'. They had made up their minds, wrote Carson to F. E. Smith, that 'the best and only solution of the question is to accept the present Bill and endeavour to work it loyally'.

The historic province of Ulster consists of nine counties. Not surprisingly there was considerable resistance within the Ulster Unionist Council to the establishment of a six-county Northern Ireland, especially from the delegates of the three excluded counties – Cavan, Donegal and Monaghan. Their exclusion, they argued, was not only a violation of the Covenant they had all signed in 1912, but a six-county unit was too small for a viable parliament, which was bound to become parochial, and the large Unionist majority that would inevitably result was 'unwise'. It was certainly true that the position both of the Unionist party and the Protestant churches would be considerably stronger in a six-county Northern Ireland than in a nine-county Ulster. If the three counties of Cavan, Donegal and Monaghan had been included in Northern Ireland, Protestants and Catholics would have been much more evenly balanced; and even if they had been able to command a majority at first, the Unionists might easily, in time, have lost control of an Ulster Parliament. As Sir James Craig said, 'The three excluded counties contain some 70,000 Sinn Feiners and Nationalists, and the addition of that large stock of Sinn Feiners and Nationalists would reduce our majority to such a level that no sane man would undertake to carry on a Parliament with it'. In those circumstances, as Thomas Moles, one of the Unionists' Belfast MPs said, 'in a sinking ship, with lifeboats sufficient for only two-thirds of the ship's company, were all to condemn themselves to death because all could not be saved?'.

The Government of Ireland Act became law on 23 November 1920. On 4 February 1921 Carson handed over the leadership of the Ulster Unionist party to Sir James Craig. On 24 May – Empire Day – the first elections for the Northern Ireland Parliament were held. 40 Unionists were returned, together with 6 Nationalists and 6 Republicans who refused to take their seats, and Craig became Northern Ireland's first prime minister. For him, as for other Unionists, the limited Home Rule conferred on Northern Ireland by the Act was far from satisfactory. 'As a final settlement and supreme sacrifice in the interests of peace, the Government of Ireland Act 1920 was accepted by Northern Ireland, although not asked for by her representatives' he wrote to Lloyd George in November 1921. That being so however, Craig believed that it was the Unionists' business to take the measure of local self-government they had been offered and make it work. 'Make it work' meant, quite simply, to ensure that the British connection – although it had been weakened – should not be weakened any further.

The connection appeared to be threatened at the very start. The opening of the Northern Ireland Parliament by King George V in June 1921 had created an opportunity for the conclusion of a truce in the Anglo-Irish war; this was followed by the protracted negotiations which ended with the signing of the Anglo-Irish Treaty on 7 December 1921. Lloyd George was afraid that the Sinn Fein delegates might use Ulster as an excuse to break off negotiations, and that if they did so, public opinion would be sympathetic to Sinn Fein. During the negotiations, therefore, he put considerable pressure on Craig to accept local autonomy for North-

ern Ireland inside an all-Ireland Parliament. Otherwise, wrote Lloyd George to Craig, 'grave difficulties would be raised for both parts of Ireland'. Craig replied that 'an all-Ireland Parliament cannot under existing circumstances be accepted by Northern Ireland', but that, as the Government of Ireland Act had provided for equal powers for both north and south, both north and south might become Dominions. 'Partition on those lines the majority of the Irish people will never accept, nor could we conscientiously attempt to enforce it', wrote back Lloyd George. 'It would be fatal to that purpose of a lasting settlement on which these negotiations from the very outset have been steadily directed.' For Northern Ireland to accept an all-Ireland Parliament, retorted Craig, 'involves the placing of Ulster under Sinn Fein, which is an insurmountable difficulty'.

Lloyd George was unable to coerce Craig, and the Sinn Fein delegates signed a Treaty which provided that Northern Ireland might opt out of an all-Ireland Parliament, but that if she did so, the border would be subject to revision by a Boundary Commission. Though the Northern Ireland government immediately exercised the right to withdraw from the Free State which the Treaty gave them, Craig protested that the automatic inclusion of Northern Ireland in the Free State was a complete reversal of the British Government's previous policy. He also declared that the Boundary Commission had been set up 'without our having previously been consulted', when Lloyd George had promised that the rights of Ulster would be 'in no way sacrificed or compromised until new proposals had been placed before the Cabinet of Northern Ireland'. The result was to leave the Ulster Unionists extremely suspicious of the British Government's intentions and to increase their already considerable fears of isolation.

There was however a more serious threat to the new government of Northern Ireland – a campaign of violence organised by the IRA. There had been a considerable amount of violence in the north during the previous two years, especially in Belfast. In July 1920, for example, Protestants in the shipyards had decided to

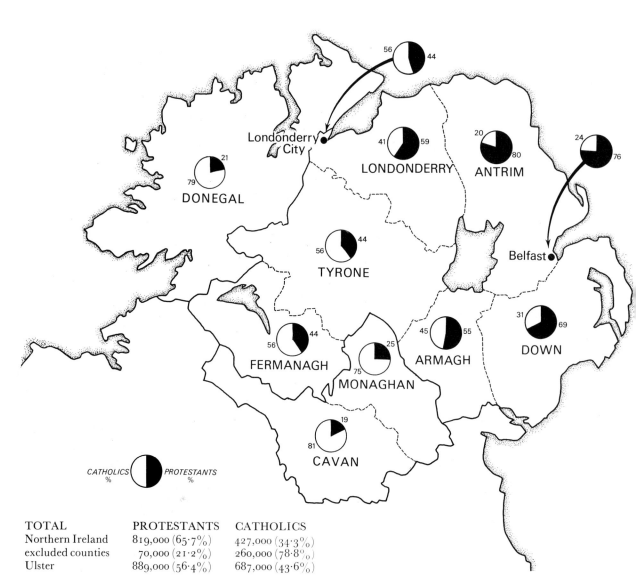

This map shows the distribution of Catholics and Protestants in the nine counties of Ulster, according to the census of 1911. In the six counties of Northern Ireland there was only one substantial change in the balance between 1911 and 1961 – in the city of Londonderry, where the proportion of Catholics increased from 56% to 67%. In all three excluded counties, on the other hand, the proportion of Protestants declined considerably during the same period.

TOTAL	PROTESTANTS	CATHOLICS
Northern Ireland	819,000 (65·7%)	427,000 (34·3%)
excluded counties	70,000 (21·2%)	260,000 (78·8%)
Ulster	889,000 (56·4%)	687,000 (43·6%)

expel their Catholic fellow-workers. In the three terrible days and nights of rioting that followed 62 people were killed, more than 200 injured and many Catholics were driven from their homes. Violence continued sporadically throughout 1921, but in the first six months of 1922 the IRA made violent efforts, both in Belfast and along the border, to prevent the

new state from functioning at all. 232 people were killed and more than 1000 injured, many in vicious sectarian reprisals, £3 million worth of property was destroyed and lasting damage was done to relations between the two communities. The outbreak of the civil war in the south in the summer of 1922 removed the immediate threat, but many on both sides contin-

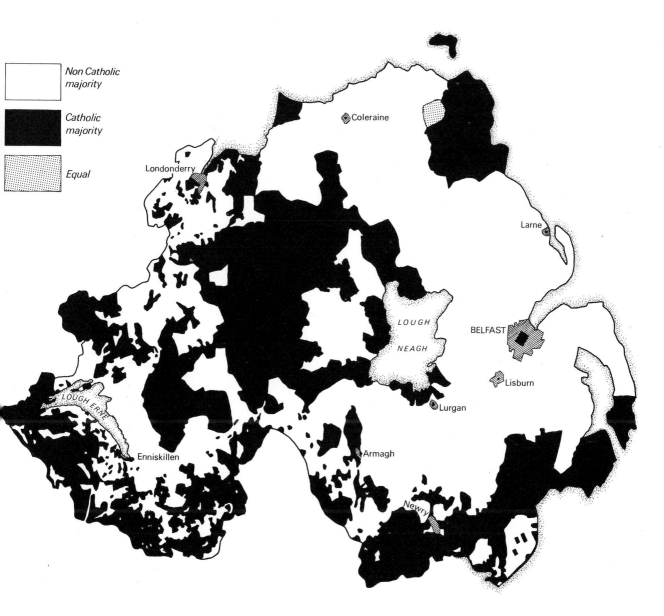

This map shows the distribution of Catholics and Protestants within the six counties which later became Northern Ireland, according to the census of 1911. In the border areas this is given by parishes, and shows the very considerable extent to which the two communities were intermingled there – quite apart from the substantial Catholic enclaves in other parts of the six counties.

Non Catholic majority

Catholic majority

Equal

Coleraine

Londonderry

Larne

LOUGH NEAGH

BELFAST

Lisburn

Lurgan

LOUGH ERNE

Enniskillen

Armagh

Newry

ued for some time – either in fear or in hope – to expect armed intervention from the south.

The long and bitter struggle to secure its authority left an enduring mark on the character of the new regime. In April 1922 the Northern Ireland Government passed the Special Powers Act, which gave the Minister of Home Affairs widespread powers 'to take all such steps and issue all such orders as may be necessary for preserving the peace' – or, in the words of one MP, 'The Home Secretary shall have power to do what he likes, or else let somebody else do what he likes for him'. In the circumstances of the time, some such temporary measure – as the Act was originally intended to be – was probably inevitable, but it continued to be renewed annually, and was made permanent in 1933; it remained in force until 1970. Since it was intended to operate against the IRA, however, the Act bore most heavily on the Catholic population, and many Catholics felt that it was operated without any pretence of impartiality. In the same way, the Ulster Special Constabulary was established in November 1920, on the basis of the old UVF, to help the government maintain law and order during the Anglo-Irish war, and it was this armed force of some 44,000 men which was largely responsible for preventing the new state from dissolving into anarchy. The Special Constabulary was however an overwhelmingly Protestant force, largely drawn from the Orange Order, and it achieved an early reputation for sectarian violence which it never afterwards lost. In 1925 the A and C platoons of the Special Constabulary were disbanded, but the B platoons – the B Specials – remained in existence until 1969. It is not surprising that – whether this was justified or not – the Special Powers Act and the B Specials together did more than anything else to blacken the subsequent reputation of the Northern Ireland authorities, especially with the Catholic minority.

More serious for the new state than the onslaught of the IRA, because it was both more permanent and more wide-ranging in its effect, was the refusal of the Catholic nationalist third[1] of the population of Northern Ireland either to recognise the new state or to play any part in its affairs during its early formative years. It was not just that their elected representatives refused to take their seats in the Northern Ireland Parliament, and that 21 local authorities, where the Nationalists were in a majority, refused to recognise that Parliament's authority, but the managers and teachers of some 300 Catholic schools refused to recognise the Northern Ireland Ministry of Education and some teachers in Co. Tyrone even refused for a time to accept their salaries from the new State. And such resistance received the official sanction of the Church. Cardinal

Logue, the Archbishop of Armagh, denounced 'the sham settlement devised by the British Government'. 'An ancient land made one by God,' protested Dr MacRory, the Bishop of Down and Connor, had been 'partitioned by a foreign power against the vehement protests of her people'.

For Catholics in Northern Ireland did not believe the new State could last. There were, after all, large areas of Northern Ireland, especially in Fermanagh and Tyrone, south Down, south Armagh and the city of Londonderry, where Catholics were in a majority. Catholics in the North believed, with Griffith and Collins, that the Boundary Commission set up by the Treaty would award so much of Northern Ireland to the Free State that Northern Ireland would be unable to survive. In the meantime there seemed little point in helping to make the new state work. In spite of the fact that Lloyd George had assured him in December 1921 that the Boundary Commission 'was only intended to make a slight adjustment of our boundary line', Craig was well aware that Lloyd George had given Collins a very different impression of the way the Boundary Commission might operate. The wording of Article XII of the Treaty was also – in spite of what Lloyd George and other ministers in his government might say – very ambiguous. Lloyd George had after all refused Northern Ireland Dominion status because it 'would stereotype a frontier based neither upon natural features nor broad geographical considerations'. Craig was adamant. 'I will never give in to any rearrangement of the boundary that leaves our Ulster area less than it is under the Government of Ireland Act' he said in the Northern Ireland Parliament in January 1922, and two months later, in a more famous and more succinct statement of his position, he declared 'What we have now we hold'. He continued to maintain that the Boundary Commission was a breach of the terms of the Government of Ireland Act, that it had been agreed to without the consent of the Northern Ireland government, and that his government was therefore not legally bound to appoint a member of the Commission. Craig's intransigence, the Civil War in the south, and

[1] Of course not *every* Catholic was a Nationalist, nor was *every* Protestant a Unionist, either in 1922, or today, but the connection is close enough to be substantially accurate.

the political instability of Britain after the fall of the Lloyd George coalition government in 1922, all meant that it was not until October 1924 that the Boundary Commission – with a member for Northern Ireland appointed by the British Government – was finally established. Craig immediately told the Northern Ireland Parliament that, if the Commission's Report was unfavourable, he would resign and take any steps that might be necessary to defend the threatened area.

In the event, the Commission – as an inspired leak to the *Morning Post* in November 1925 suggested – proposed only minor adjustments to the boundary. Since both the British and the Free State governments feared that widespread violence might follow if the Commission's recommendations were accepted, a Tripartite Agreement was signed with the government of Northern Ireland on 3 December 1925, in which the three governments, 'being resolved mutually to aid one another in a spirit of neighbourly comradeship', agreed to recognise the existing boundary.

But the long delay in appointing the Commission had left the Catholic Nationalist minority in Northern Ireland in a very vulnerable position and, when all three governments agreed to bury the Commission's Report, their demoralisation was complete. 'It is a betrayal of the Nationalists of the North,' said Cahir Healy, 'and a denial of every statement put forward by the Free State in their alleged support of our cause since 1921.' Some clung to the hope that the IRA would come to their rescue, but since by 1925 the IRA was almost equally demoralised by its defeat in the Civil War, there was nothing left for the minority in the north but to learn to live with the situation.

After 1925 the Nationalists began to come back into politics, led – for the last few years of his life – by the veteran Joe Devlin. But by then the damage was done. By 1925 the events of the last few years had only confirmed the widespread view among Protestants in Northern Ireland that *all* Catholics were rebels and that they had demonstrated by their behaviour both their fundamental disloyalty and their unfitness to be associated in the running of the State. They had shown

themselves to be unwilling citizens; no one therefore need have any compunction about making them second-class citizens.

Although the Unionists dominated the Northern Ireland Parliament[2] – they never won less than 33 of the 52 seats in the House of Commons and the combined strength of all parties committed to maintaining the British connection was never less than 40 – this dominance merely reflected the size of the Protestant majority in the six counties; the existence of a business vote and 4 university seats until 1969 (both were abolished in Britain in 1948) gave them only a marginal advantage. And though the abolition of proportional representation at Stormont in 1929 certainly helped to maintain party discipline, it had little effect on the pattern of representation in the House.

But the Unionists' position in local government was less secure. In 1921 many authorities were controlled by the Nationalists. In 1922 proportional representation in local government was abolished, local government boundaries were re-drawn, and the immediate result in many cases was to convert what had formerly been a Nationalist majority into a Unionist majority. In Co. Fermanagh, for example, the Nationalists had controlled five of the seven local authorities in 1921. In 1922 the Unionists had majorities in three of the four new authorities. 'When the government of Northern Ireland decided to do away with proportional representation,' said W. T. Millar, one of the local Unionist MPs, 'the chance that we had been waiting for, for so long, arrived. We took advantage. We divided the country in the way that we thought best.'

Such gerrymandering – the deliberate manipulation of local government electoral boundaries in order to achieve and maintain control of local authorities – was one of the major complaints of discrimination against the Catholic Nationalist minority investigated by the Cameron Commission in 1969. This was not new, however; a study of Northern Ireland published in

[2] Usually referred to as the Stormont Parliament, from the area outside Belfast where the Parliament building stands.

1935 concluded that 'a scrutiny of the redistribution of areas carried out by the Government reveals that there does exist very considerable justification for the complaints of the minority'. The most glaring example – in the words of the Cameron Commission – was the County Borough of Londonderry. Here, by the manipulation of ward boundaries, a Protestant minority of 8,781 voters, largely concentrated in two wards, returned 12 Unionists to the City Council, and a Catholic majority of 14,429, largely concentrated in one ward, returned 8 Nationalists. Both in Londonderry, and in several other areas, such a situation had been perpetuated, concluded the Cameron Commission, by the allocation of local authority housing, so that the Catholic population was effectively confined to the wards where there was already a Catholic majority. As one Unionist said, in Co. Fermanagh: 'We are going to see that the right people are put into these houses, and we are not making any apologies for it'.

It was not, furthermore, until 1969 that the principle of one man, one vote, applied to local government elections in Northern Ireland.[3] The franchise – restricted largely to rate-payers and heavily weighted in favour of property – resulted in the exclusion of about a quarter of the electorate: nearly 7,000 of the 30,000 voters in Londonderry, for example, could not vote in local elections. This restriction undoubtedly operated against the poorer – Catholic – section of the population, though without the readjustment of boundaries the extension of the franchise would have had little effect on the composition of local authorities.

The Cameron Commission concluded, finally, that Unionist-controlled councils in several areas had also used their powers to make appointments in a way that benefited Protestants. In 1968, for example, only 30 per cent of the administrative, clerical and technical employees of Londonderry Corporation were Catholics, though Catholics formed 60 per cent of the population.[4] The justification for this degree of discrimination has always been that the Catholic Nationalist minority is fundamentally disloyal. 'The Northern government is a Protestant government, put into power

by Protestants, and the welfare and safety of the Protestants should be its first consideration' said Senator Porter-Porter in 1931. 'Catholics are out to destroy Ulster with all their might and power' said Sir Basil Brooke in 1933. 'They want to nullify the Protestant vote, take all they can out of Ulster, and then see it go to hell.' When the Prime Minister was challenged to say whether he accepted what Brooke (then his Minister of Agriculture) had said, Craig, now Viscount Craigavon, replied: 'I would not ask him to withdraw one word of it and there is not one of my colleagues who does not agree with what he said'. Indeed, Craig himself, had made several similar statements – notably in 1934, when he declared: 'All I boast of is that we are a Protestant Parliament and a Protestant State'.

Such language is sometimes dismissed as mindless fanaticism. It must however be remembered first that not only was the Catholic Nationalist minority excluded from power because they could never hope to form a government, they could never hope to form an official opposition either;[5] they were, after all, concerned to destroy the British connection and bring about the reunification of Ireland. And, under pressure both from their own and from Protestant extremists, the Nationalists continued to reserve the right to 'come in or stay outside [parliament] as and when our people may decide'. Such an attitude appeared to many Unionists to justify the permanent exclusion of the minority from any share in government – though the economic depression of the 1930s probably contributed to the intemperance with which leading politicians expressed this view.

Far more significant in helping to maintain what can only be called the siege mentality of the Protestant Unionist majority in Northern Ireland, however, has been the attitude of successive Dublin governments.

[3] Once again, Northern Ireland retained the system that had existed in Great Britain down to the post-war reforms.
[4] It is only fair to point out however (as the Cameron Commission also did) that the same thing applied to the Protestant minority in the few local authorities run by the Nationalists.
[5] They did agree to do so in 1965, after the O'Neill-Lemass meetings (see p. 101).

Neither the Free State nor the Republic has ever fully recognised the existence of Northern Ireland, and there were continual declarations fron southern politicians along the lines that 'no claim to separation from Ireland can be substantiated by any section of the Irish people'. De Valera's success in severing the Imperial connection with Britain during the 1930's was regarded with increasing suspicion and hostility in the north, especially after the claims made in his 1937 constitution that 'the national territory consists of the whole island of Ireland' but that 'pending the re-integration of the national territory' it would only apply to the 26 counties. The result was that, in the 1938 election in Northern Ireland, the Unionists gained 3 seats and the next Parliament contained the largest number of Union supporters ever to be elected to Stormont.

The events of 1948 and 1949 underlined the connection even more strongly. In 1948, when the Dublin government announced its intention of establishing an Irish Republic and the British government acquiesced, Sir Basil Brooke – now Prime Minister of Northern Ireland – declared: 'The people of Ulster feel that this final step of the Eire government is the vindication of the decision to which we have adhered through many troubled and difficult years: to move not an inch towards compromise with a people whose historic associations and political loyalties are so different from our own'. When, during the 1949 election campaign in Northern Ireland, collections were made outside churches in the south to assist opposition candidates, Brooke condemned such 'unjustifiable interference' and when Costello and de Valera, the leaders of the two major political parties in the south, made a joint protest against partition, Brooke denounced their claim to Irish unity as 'monstrous'. 'Our country is in danger', said Brooke in his final election message; 'Today we fight to defend our very existence and the heritage of our Ulster children.' The result was a sharp increase in many Unionist majorities, and in Belfast the party gained three seats from Labour, Brooke having rightly predicted that 'the Unionist people will give no backing to candidates who belong to a party which is undecided about such a vital issue'.

The British Prime Minister, Clement Atlee, had twice stated in the House of Commons that when Eire became a Republic there could be no change in the constitutional status of Northern Ireland without Northern Ireland's agreement, and the Ireland Act of May 1949 contained the following clause: 'It is hereby declared that Northern Ireland remains part of His Majesty's dominions and of the United Kingdom and it is hereby affirmed that in no event will Northern Ireland or any part thereof cease to be a part of His Majesty's dominions and of the United Kingdom, without the consent of the Parliament of Northern Ireland.' The immediate reaction from Dublin was the tabling of a motion in the Dail by the Taoiseach, J. A. Costello, protesting 'against the introduction in the British Parliament of legislation purporting to endorse and continue the existing partition of Ireland'. A few days later, an all-party Anti-Partition conference called on the British Government and people 'to end the present occupation of our six north-eastern counties' and Mr Costello demanded the return of Fermanagh, Tyrone, south Armagh and Londonderry city 'as a first instalment of our rights'.

Ulster Unionism is not naturally monolithic. There always have been, and still are, antagonisms of class and of religion within Unionist ranks. But these discords were immediately silenced at election after election by the simple warning that the Union was in danger. The effect of this message has depended less on the positive advantages of Union than on the alarm that the attitude of successive Dublin governments has aroused among rank and file Unionists.[6]

If any further explanation of this alarm were needed, it has been provided by the IRA; by the fluctuating, but occasionally considerable, electoral support for its political wing, Sinn Fein; and by the ambiguous attitude of the Catholic population, north and south of the border, to both organisations. For thirty years after

[6] For the connection between this and the influence of the Roman Catholic church, see chapter 10 (pp. 122–129).

their withdrawal south for the Civil War, the militants in the north were about as effective as the Fenians had been in the early years of the century. Though the movement failed dismally in its declared intention to liberate the six counties, the border campaign of 1956–62 and occasional violence at other times (especially during the Second World War) had an important influence on maintaining Unionist solidarity.

The maintenance of Unionist solidarity has also been positively assisted by the connections, both official and unofficial, between the Unionist party, the Protestant churches, and the Orange Order. And it has been cemented by the widespread segregation of Catholics and Protestants in housing, education and employment – a segregation that cut so deep that, as a recent examination of the Northern Ireland problem reported: 'Many have no need to go farther than an idea of the other community as "they"'.

During the depression of the 1930s, social and economic distress added to the existing political rivalries between the two communities. Given that there was discrimination already, discrimination in a cold climate was bound to reinforce the resentment of Catholics, who inevitably found themselves at the end of the queue.[7] Northern Ireland was particularly badly hit because of its dependence on the declining industries of linen and shipbuilding. Throughout the 1930s between 23 and 28 per cent of the insured population – between 63,000 and 84,000 people – were unemployed, and the financial resources then available to the Northern Ireland government were wholly inadequate either for dealing with the human distress caused by the depression, or for carrying out the kind of long-term reforms that would prevent a similar disaster in the future. In 1932 there was a remarkable demonstration in which unemployed Protestants in the Shankill Road in Belfast rioted in support of unemployed Catholics in the Falls Road who had been attacked by the police. But the traditional appeal to sectarian loyalties soon re-asserted itself; in the summer of 1935 11 people

were killed and 600 injured in some of the worst riots ever seen in Belfast.

Three main issues had dominated life in Northern Ireland in the 1920s and 1930s – the maintenance of the British connection, the deep divisions between Protestant and Catholic, Unionist and Nationalist, and the increasing problem of keeping a declining economy afloat. But the context in which all these problems was discussed was dramatically changed by the Second World War, when Northern Ireland became vital to the very existence of the United Kingdom. In 1938 de Valera had negotiated with Chamberlain for the return of naval bases in the south which Britain had retained under the terms of the Anglo-Irish Treaty, and as a result Eire was able to remain neutral throughout the war. But in the absence of these bases, the northern ports played a crucial role in the battle of the Atlantic. 'But for the loyalty of Northern Ireland,' said Winston Churchill in 1943, 'we should have been confronted with slavery and death, and the light which now shines so strongly throughout the world would have been quenched.' Nor was that all. The area under cultivation was doubled, more than 170 warships were built in Belfast and Northern Ireland became the training ground for 120,000 American troops. 'Without Northern Ireland,' said General Eisenhower, 'I do not see how the American forces could have been concentrated to begin the invasion of Europe.' All this meant that unemployment fell sharply and average incomes more than doubled, with dramatic effects both on the standard of living and on people's expectations for the future.

Northern Ireland's contribution to the war effort undoubtedly helped Sir Basil Brooke to secure the recognition of Northern Ireland's special position in the Ireland Act of 1949. And, which was perhaps more important, it helped the Northern Ireland government to establish that, in order for the six counties to maintain parity with the rest of the United Kingdom in the enormous expansion of social services that took place in the years after the war, the British Government would have to provide Northern Ireland with large and con-

[7] The economic history of this period is dealt with in chapter 8 (pp. 102–109).

tinuing subsidies – subsidies which have now reached an annual level of more than £160 million.

This massive increase in government spending after the war, and the considerable increase in investment both by the government and by private industry, maintained the improvement in the economic climate that had begun during the war. A Catholic population which had received what they regarded as their fair share of this improvement might, in time, have come to accept, and to participate, in the system. A few did; a few more became increasingly alienated; many simply acquiesced. In any case, said Professor Thomas Wilson in a survey of Northern Ireland published in 1955, the Catholic Nationalist minority 'have less to complain about than the US negroes and their lot is a very pleasant one as compared with that of the nationalists in, say, the Ukraine'. The major issue for the Protestant Unionist majority remained the British connection, and their instinct was to insist that, as Catholics could not be trusted to work the system, they could not be fully admitted to its benefits. Sir Basil Brooke, created Viscount Brookeborough in 1952, was Prime Minister of Northern Ireland for twenty years, from 1943 to 1963, and shared the general belief of his supporters in the paramount necessity of maintaining the status quo. 'The fact is that the Roman Catholic, by and large, is out to destroy Ulster and bring it into a United Ireland', he said to me. 'The Protestant is out to maintain Northern Ireland's position within the United Kingdom.'

Lord Brookeborough's successor, Captain Terence O'Neill, did not share this traditional view and made a determined effort to bridge the gulf both between the two communities in Northern Ireland and between Ireland and the Republic – a new departure dramatised by his exchange of visits with Sean Lemass, the Taoiseach of the Irish Republic, in 1965. In Unionist terms, O'Neill's philosophy was revolutionary: 'Here we are, in this small country of ours, Protestant and Catholic, committed by history to live side by side. No solution based on the ascendancy of any section of our community can hope to endure. Either we live in peace, or we have no life worth living.'

But even the relatively timid attempts which O'Neill made to build on the atmosphere of detente, an atmosphere which he had helped to create, were too radical a breach with tradition for his own party. Any serious change in the status quo was bound to arouse considerable opposition in the Protestant, Unionist majority. On the other hand, the expectations of the Catholic, Nationalist minority had been aroused. If these expectations were disappointed there was bound to be an equally strong reaction. When the explosion came, therefore, it was due less to a sense of hopelessness than to a sense of great expectations imperfectly fulfilled.

WHEN THE BOUGH BREAKS

'We find in Ulster,' wrote J. W. Woodburn in his book *The Ulster Scot* in 1915, 'the largest linen manufactory, the largest ship-building yard, the largest rope-making factory, the largest tobacco factory and the largest mineral water factory in the world. The success of the people of Belfast in these things is a striking proof of what energy and perseverance can accomplish. The city of Belfast has few natural advantages, for it has to import every pound of iron and every ton of coal, and yet the spirit and enterprise of the Ulsterman have enabled him to surmount these obstacles'.

For Unionists the British connection was vital to their prosperity, and one of the major reasons for the opposition to Home Rule had been the fear that this prosperity would be destroyed in an independent Ireland. For Nationalists, on the other hand, the British connection was seen, not as the vital link on which their prosperity depended, but as the major barrier in the way of achieving it. 'We have in Ireland all the resources necessary to build up a thriving community', wrote the author of a survey of Irish industry published in 1920. 'Endless proof is available of the ability of Irishmen to cope successfully with economic problems; our workpeople are comparable with those of any other nation, both in regard to skill and intelligence; all that we lack to enable us to take our proper place among the prosperous nations of the world is the power to determine our own economic policy'. It was for this reason that Arthur Griffith had put economic self-sufficiency at the heart of the Sinn Fein programme: 'A nation cannot promote and further its civilisation and its social progress equally as well by exchanging agricultural products for manufactured goods as by establishing a manufacturing power of its own'.

It might have been expected therefore that, when an independent Irish government raised on Griffith's ideas at last came to power in 1922, it should have put these ideas into practice. But 90 per cent of the Free State's exports still went to the United Kingdom and the Irish pound was tied to sterling; economic independence was only possible if the population of the Free State was prepared to accept a considerable fall in its standard of living. Inevitably, in the face of harsh reality, the Cosgrave government rejected the pure gospel of Sinn Fein. It was Kevin O'Higgins who disposed of Griffith in one devastating sentence. 'The propagandist political writings of one man,' he declared, 'cannot be accepted as revealed truth, requiring no further investigation, something that must be accepted for ever as beyond question, beyond doubt, beyond the need of examination'.

Examination of course revealed that the Free State had few industries and fewer raw materials, and that agriculture was – and would long remain – the country's most important industry. The main aim of the government's policy therefore was to make farmers prosperous, for without their prosperity there would be no market for Irish industry. Moreover, without the export earnings of Irish agriculture, there would be no money to import the raw materials without which Irish industry could not operate. As so much of what was produced on the farms – livestock and dairy produce – was exported, the government's policy should be to encourage this specialisation, to improve the quality of the product and to keep production costs down. This was particularly important since the reputation of those exports had been damaged by the rush to take advantage of the quick profits to be made out of exporting food to Britain during the 1914-18 war. Indeed the new peasant proprietor – who had only recently emerged victorious from the Land War – had now to be fitted for a more competitive existence.

As for industry, the government's attitude was to be resolutely pragmatic: 'The Government takes up no doctrinaire attitude on the question of free trade and protection. It regards the matter as one of expediency'. Expediency dictated a cautious, almost disapproving, attitude to protection in which the onus of proof that protection was necessary was placed on the applicant; the result was that the list of protected commodities was small and relatively unimportant.

By 1932, when the Cosgrave government was succeeded by De Valera's first Fianna Fail administration, the world depression was already making an economic policy based on exporting agricultural products and importing industrial goods virtually impossible. At first the Free State was little affected, but as tariff barriers went up round the world Ireland had little option but to follow suit. Even without the international crisis however the new government would have followed a much more nationalist policy – a policy already outlined in 1928 by Sean Lemass, who was now Fianna Fail's first Minister for Industry and Commerce: 'We believe that Ireland can be made a self-contained unit providing all the necessities of living in adequate quantities for the people residing in the island at the moment and probably for a much larger number'. There were strong moral overtones in this drive for self-sufficiency, which reflected de Valera's conviction that the country ought to achieve real economic independence whatever the cost, and his strong belief in the traditional virtues of Irish rural society: 'I am not satisfied that the standard of living and the mode of life in western Europe is a right or proper one,' he said, 'the industrialised countries have got themselves into a rut and Ireland is asked to hurry along it after them'.

Since a vast proportion of Irish trade was still with the United Kingdom this new policy would in any case have made relations with Britain more difficult. But when he took office, de Valera also declared that his government would no longer collect and pay over to the British government the land annuities created under the Wyndham Act of 1903 and subsequent legislation – the capital repayments and the interest on the capital loaned to Irish farmers by the British government so that they could buy their land.[1] The British government promptly retaliated, first by levying a 20 per cent duty (which was later increased), and then by imposing quotas, on all Irish cattle imports. The Free State government in return put duties on British imports – especially coal, steel, cement and machinery. So began the 'economic war' which – though it was modified by a series of Cattle/Coal pacts after January 1935, lasted until 1938, when the Free State government paid £10 million as 'a final settlement of all financial claims of either of the two governments against each other' (– a highly advantageous bargain for the Irish, since the annuities were worth about £3 million/year and many still had 30 years to run).

The main victim of the economic war was the Irish economy. The value of Irish exports fell from nearly £36 million in 1929 to just under £18 million in 1935, and even though prices were falling during the depression, this was still a considerable decline. More significantly, the number of cattle exported from the Free State to Britain fell by nearly a third between 1929 and 1935 and the cattle industry in Ireland was almost ruined. But the most serious consequence of the economic war was that, since it had such a disastrous effect on farm incomes (which fell from £32 million in 1929/30 to £14 million in 1933), the potential market for the new industries which were being created at the same time was drastically reduced.

The Fianna Fail government however did not hesitate. It raised Irish tariffs, so that by 1936 more than 2,000 separate items were subject to import duty, and the average level of this duty rose from 9 per cent to 35 per cent, the fifth highest tariff in the world. Behind this barrier the government did everything it could to develop native Irish industries. Though some tariffs were raised on the government's own initiative – like that on cars – most were raised at the request of individual entrepreneurs. As the secretary of the Department of Industry and Commerce recalled: 'Broadly speaking, the attitude of the government was that any firm or group of firms or individuals prepared to establish a new industry, or to extend an existing industry, could make application for the grant of the duties necessary to give ample protection, and so create conditions in which external competition was to a large extent eliminated'. The Control of Manufactures Acts (1932/4) laid down that a majority of any company's directors

[1] The transfer of land, which was not quite finished by the time of the Treaty, had been completed by compulsory purchase in 1923; though some tenants, who did not wish to buy their land, continued to pay rent to the government.

should be Irish and that two-thirds of the voting capital should be in Irish hands, for otherwise 'new industries would be almost exclusively in the hands of foreigners'. In 1933 an Industrial Credit Corporation was established to help finance the transfer of capital to Irish hands and in four years more than £6 million was advanced for this purpose.

Perhaps the most significant development of the period however was the launching of a number of what have come to be called state-sponsored bodies. Even under the Cosgrave government, which took an almost Victorian view of the functions of government – it kept taxation deliberately low and spent very little on social welfare – the state had begun to intervene in the workings of the economy. This was probably inevitable since, even if private capital in Ireland had not been both limited and unenterprising (even before independence most of it had been invested abroad) the Irish economy was both too small and too poor to attract much private investment. This was especially true in areas which, although they were essential for the country's economic development, required a great deal of capital and promised a very uncertain return.

Probably the most spectacular of these ventures was the Electricity Supply Board, established in 1927. The ESB was based on a scheme to harness the waters of the river Shannon to provide 110 million units of electricity a year. Within ten years the ESB were generating over 400 million units, and the programme of rural electrification begun after the Shannon scheme has done more to change the face of rural Ireland than almost anything else. Between 1932 and 1945 eighteen new semi-state industries were established, either replacing the failures of private enterprise (like the Irish steel corporation) or developing areas it had ignored (like the processing of peat into fuel), and by the mid 1960s there were 34 of these 'trading enterprises'. In the course of time therefore a characteristically Irish paradox emerged – one of the most resolutely anti-socialist countries in the world was also the country where a form of state socialism rapidly became central to the development of the economy.

The immediate effects of de Valera's policy of economic self-sufficiency were not very startling. True, between 1931 and 1938 net industrial output rose from just under £26 million to £36 million and the numbers employed in industry rose from 111,000 to 166,000. Against this, however, the few large industries that already existed – like whiskey, stout and biscuits – suffered because they relied primarily on exports, and the new industries were expensive to run, sometimes inefficiently managed and too small to compete successfully abroad. Not only therefore did they make very little contribution to exports, they also used imported raw materials and so helped to increase the balance of payments deficit. Although these new industries failed to make the impact on the Irish economy that the de Valera government had expected however they created a pool of skilled labour and managerial experience – and perhaps more important, they established several basic industries without which Ireland could never have survived during the Second World War.

This was even more true of agriculture. The aim of the Fianna Fail government, as described by the secretary of the Department of Agriculture in 1935, was to make the country 'self-sufficient in respect of all agricultural commodities for the production of which the soil and climate are suitable, or for which suitable substitutes can be grown in the country'. The implication of this policy was that the existing preoccupation with livestock and dairy produce should be abandoned and efforts concentrated on the encouragement of tillage, especially of wheat. In normal circumstances such a policy would have been contrary both to what was geographically most appropriate and to what was economically most profitable, but in the circumstances of the 1930s – even without the dislocation caused by the economic war – some adjustment of the pattern of agricultural production would have been necessary. Though the results of the tillage drive were not very impressive – only 67,000 out of 8 million acres were transferred from pasture to tillage between 1931 and 1939 – the fact that, within the area under tillage, the acreage under wheat rose from 21,000 acres in 1931 to

255,000 acres in 1936 was, during the war, to make all the difference between life and death.

The war of course put even more emphasis on the policy of self-sufficiency. In doing so, however, it also emphasised the inherent weakness of the Irish economy. Though, by distorting the traditional pattern of Irish agriculture even more, the Free State managed to harvest 662,000 acres of wheat in 1945 – the largest figure since statistics began in 1847 – and though meat exports to Britain built up substantial reserves of sterling, industrial development was almost at a standstill; indeed it appears that between 1939 and 1947 economic growth in the Free State was *nil*.

After the war both agriculture and industry revived, and for several years the economy expanded at about 5 per cent a year. In spite of considerable government assistance however, sustained economic growth could not be achieved. The rate of expansion fell back below 2 per cent in the early '50s, and by 1956 the sterling balances accumulated during the war had been exhausted. In the thirty-five years between 1921 and 1956 economic growth had averaged 1 per cent a year, and at the end Ireland was in the throes of an economic crisis.

Worse even than this, emigration began to increase at an alarming rate. Between 1936 and 1946 there was a net fall of 187,000 in the Free State's population, and a further 120,000 left between 1946 and 1951. In the early 1950s, the attraction of higher wages and better living conditions in Britain began to become irresistible. By 1954 emigration was running at the rate of 40,000 a year, figures unknown since the end of the nineteenth century. As the government's Commission on Emigration reported in 1955: 'Emigration has been due to two fundamental causes – the absence of opportunities for making an adequate livelihood, and a growing desire for higher standards of living on the part of the community, particularly the rural community'. It began to seem to many that, in the traditional words of the emigrant, 'this country is finished' and that there would be a flight from the land comparable to that which had taken place in the years after the Famine.

The result was that a Capital Investment Advisory Committee, appointed in 1955, demanded a programme for economic expansion. This programme was drawn up by T. K. Whitaker, secretary of the Department of Finance and his report, *Economic Development*, published in November 1958, may be said to have marked a watershed in the economic history of the Republic.

'We now lag so far behind most other European countries in material progress that even a spectacular increase in efficiency and output will leave us at a relative disadvantage' concluded Whitaker. 'If we are to catch up at all, our rate of improvement must exceed theirs.' The report recognised that: 'The fortunes of all sections of agriculture are linked to livestock production and the general prosperity of the economy is associated with the cattle export trade', but the main emphasis was on industry. Here the primary aim was to stimulate 'a vast increase in private industrial development while maintaining the supply of capital for productive state enterprises'. From this followed two conclusions, both of which have since become of major importance. The first was that, since 'Investment in Ireland has for years been insufficient to ensure economic progress at even the average rate for the rest of Europe', the most strenuous efforts would have to be made to attract foreign capital to Ireland. The second was that the old concept of self-sufficiency – whilst it had served a useful purpose in its time – was now to be abandoned. 'It is obviously essential not only that existing industries should become progressively more efficient, but also that new industries should be competitive in export markets.' The government adopted the five-year development programme proposed by Whitaker's report with only minor modifications, and Sean Lemass (who had been Minister of Industry and Commerce for 22 of the last 26 years, and who was now Taoiseach) acknowledged that 'There is need now to raise our targets and I believe also to change our methods'.

The early results were remarkable. Between 1958 and 1963, national output increased by nearly a quarter, exports rose 40 per cent and the volume of investment almost doubled. At the same time unemployment fell by a third, the purchasing power of wages rose by 20 per cent, and emigration fell, so that for the first time for more than 100 years[2] the population actually began to rise again. But agriculture hardly expanded at all, and the expansion of industry was probably due as much to the boom conditions of the early '60s as to the intentions of the first programme; the psychological effect of this sudden change in economic fortune was however considerable.

The first programme was followed by a second programme, which was to run from 1963 to 1970. Almost at once the second programme began to run into difficulties. This was due partly to the 15 per cent import levy imposed by the British government during the balance of payments crisis in 1964. Though these restrictions were later progressively removed by the Anglo-Irish Free Trade agreement of 1965, the incident showed just how closely the Irish economy was still tied to the British, and in particular how much the Irish economy still relied on agricultural exports.[3]

And though industrial development still continued, in the less favourable world economic climate of the later 1960s the Irish economy – with its dependence on exports – could not meet the optimistic targets set in the second programme. As a result the second programme was brought to a premature end and replaced by a third, and supposedly more realistic, programme, for the period 1969–72.

Nevertheless, between 1958 and 1970 44,000 new jobs were created, £150 million were invested in Irish industry, most of it by foreign-based companies, and exports more than trebled. The government have also had considerable success in persuading companies to set up factories in parts of the country where there has never been any industry before – especially in the far west. The continuing crisis in Northern Ireland and the doubts surrounding entry into the Common Market mean, however, that the future outlook is still uncertain. Above all it remains true that economic independence, which the founding fathers of the Free State believed would inevitably accompany political independence, has still not been achieved, and may indeed be unattainable.

The most obvious difference in the economic status of Northern Ireland at the time of partition, as compared with that of the Free State, was of course the intimacy of the British connection. But this difference, which now seems so crucial, was not always so obvious. As a result of the financial settlement imposed on Northern Ireland under the terms of the Government of Ireland Act in 1920, the Stormont government had no control over its principal sources of revenue and had to pay an 'imperial contribution' for services received from the United Kingdom (notably defence). At the same time, however, it had to try to secure for its people the same standard of social welfare as that provided in Britain. As a result Northern Ireland floundered about in the throes of almost continual financial crisis until, in 1938, it was agreed that the British government would make good any budget deficit, provided that this was not caused either by a lower level of taxation, or by a higher standard of social welfare, than in the rest of the United Kingdom. It can hardly be coincidental that this agreement was signed only a few days after the return of the Treaty ports to the Free State.

This hand to mouth existence meant that, though they did what they could, the Northern Ireland government was unable to provide financial assistance on the scale necessary either to modernise their agriculture or to restructure their industry. Agriculture was – and has remained – more important in the Northern Ireland economy than is often realised; in 1926 just over a quarter of the labour force worked on the land and in

[2] The population had risen by about 5,000 between 1946 and 1951, but had then continued to fall for the next ten years.

[3] Though the agricultural labour force, which was over half the working population in 1926, has now fallen to under 30 per cent of the total, and though the contribution of agriculture to the national income – which was double that of industry in 1926 – is now less than 20 per cent of the total, the *export capacity* of agriculture, and especially of the cattle trade, continues to be very important. In 1969 agricultural exports still accounted for 46 per cent of all exports. Again, though the number of large farms is continually increasing, almost half of all farms are still under 30 acres, and more than two-thirds under 50 acres.

1945 the percentage was almost exactly the same. As in the Free State, the typical unit was the family farm and – as in the Free State – the Northern Ireland government completed the transfer of land begun at the end of the previous century, and devoted much of its efforts thereafter to improving the quality of farm products and the level of agricultural education. Nevertheless, the Babington Committee reported in 1947 that: 'It is no exaggeration to say that in many parts of Ulster today farmers and labourers are working with implements that show little, if any, advance on those in use a century ago.' As in the Free State the trend was towards fewer and larger farms, but almost two thirds of the farms in the north were still under 30 acres in 1937 – about 8 per cent more than in the Free State – and less than 5 per cent were larger than 100 acres, compared with nearly 9 per cent in the south; in 1945 the average farm size in Northern Ireland was still only 36 acres. Again, as in the Free State, farmers in Northern Ireland concentrated on livestock and dairy produce, but they were able to continue selling them in Great Britain during the 1930s and did not, therefore, suffer the hardships imposed by the Economic War on farmers in the south. As a result agricultural output did rise slowly but steadily and emigration off the land was very much lower than in the south.

Though agriculture was still the largest employer in Northern Ireland, its economic survival depended on the fate of the great industries which had been a major reason for the islands partition – linen and shipbuilding. The economy was still based on these traditional industries; even in the early 1950s they employed more than half the labour force. What is more, about 60 per cent of this labour force was concentrated in Belfast and 80 per cent within thirty miles of the city. During the 1920s the prosperity of both linen and shipbuilding continued, but in the early 1930s the weaknesses that were already apparent before 1914 reappeared with even greater force as the world-wide wave of protectionism cut off the overseas markets on which both industries depended. The position in shipbuilding was particularly serious. In three years employment in the yards fell by 85 per cent; Harland & Wolff launched no ships at all in either 1932 or 1933, and in 1934 Workman and Clark went out of business altogether. Increasing competition from other fabrics meant that linen never again recovered its former position and in the summer of 1938 more than half the industry's labour force was still unemployed. The government did what it could, and between 1932 and 1939 a series of measures were passed providing loans to keep existing industries – especially Harland & Wolff – in business and offering financial inducements to attract new industry. This initiative met with a very limited response however; even by the mid 1950s it had only resulted in the creation of 6,000 new jobs. Massive unemployment – often rising above 25 per cent of the insured population – remained the sombre rule.

All this was changed by the Second World War. Employment was suddenly there for the taking – the war provided 13,000 extra jobs in the shipyards, 12,000 in the engineering works, 18,000 in Short & Harland's new aircraft factory (which had moved to Belfast in 1938). An extra 400,000 acres were put under the plough between 1939 and 1943 and the number of tractors – there were only about 550 before the war – increased to 7,700 by 1945. On the back of this wartime boom, earnings, savings and Northern Ireland's contributions to the British Exchequer all increased dramatically.

In 1945 Northern Ireland secured from the British government recognition not only of the principle that social services in Northern Ireland should be on the same level as in the rest of the United Kingdom, but also that Northern Ireland should be allowed to make up the 'leeway' it had lost between the wars. This meant that, at the very moment when the foundations of the welfare state were being laid, an extra wing was planned for Northern Ireland, and the effect on health, housing and education in particular were very considerable. It also meant the provision of a large subsidy by the British government – estimated as £45 million in the early 1960s, £121 million in 1967/68 and £235 million in 1971/72. (Admittedly this last figure includes

£85 million which would be due if Northern Ireland were still paying an Imperial Contribution – this is now a nominal £1 million – but if British subsidies were cut off and existing standards of social welfare maintained, this would cost about £160 million a year.) It was recently estimated that if the same standards applied in the Republic government expenditure would have to be more than doubled, and that if the Republic were, in addition, to continue to subsidise Northern Ireland at the present level this would require taxation in the Republic to be raised by 60 per cent.

In spite of the yawning gap between Northern Ireland and the Republic which this created, the economic position of the six counties remained fundamentally weak. Some of the impetus of the wartime boom was carried over into the first few years of peace. This was particularly true of agriculture, where the system of guaranteed prices and markets established by the Agriculture Act of 1947 gave the farmer in Northern Ireland a firm base for the expansion of production; and this has since taken place to the accompaniment of increasing mechanisation, specialisation and the consolidation of holdings. Nevertheless, though the agricultural labour force has fallen from 25 per cent of the total in 1945 to less than 10 per cent in 1970, and the number of farms has more than halved during the same period, two-thirds of all farms are still under 50 acres, and the average farm has only increased in size from 36 acres in 1945 to 48 acres in 1968; in the rest of the United Kingdom less than 10 per cent of all farms are smaller than 50 acres and the average size is 85 acres. Indeed agricultural subsidies are now virtually equivalent to the whole of farmers' incomes, and it remains to be seen, in the words of the 1970/75 development programme, 'whether appropriate changes can be carried out in farming which will raise incomes without adding unduly to the bill for subsidies and will achieve greater efficiency without unacceptable social costs'.

The problem of industry has been more intractable. As soon as the euphoria of the wartime boom had died away the same weaknesses reappeared and the familiar bogey of unemployment began once more to haunt the linen mills and the shipyards. For twenty years after the war unemployment never fell below 5 per cent and was frequently considerably higher; it has always been consistently above the British average and consistently higher than in any region in Great Britain, 'an unhappy situation which has received much attention over the years from both official and private investigators.'

Unemployment however would have been much worse without massive government assistance. By a series of Acts of Parliament something like £320 million has been pumped into the economy in grants and loans. Existing industries have benefited – the linen industry has been re-equipped and re-organised, Harland & Wolff have had loans to help with the increasing costs of modernisation. But more important than this, there has been a substantial diversification of industry and industrial production has expanded faster than in the rest of the United Kingdom – by 50 per cent between 1950 and 1962 (against 36 per cent in the UK) and by 46 per cent between 1960 and 1968 (against 24 per cent in the UK). Since the war an estimated 90,000 new jobs have been created. But at the same time traditional industries have also been contracting and many people have left the land; the net result has been that to make any impact on the unemployment figures thousands of new jobs must continue to be created every year. The extent of the problem is indicated by the 1969 review of the six-year development plan started in 1964: 'In manufacturing industry a total of almost 29,000 new jobs had been created by the end of 1969 compared with the target of 30,000. However, the run-down of employment opportunities in the older industries was sufficiently large to offset this and the net improvement in manufacturing employment was only 5000 jobs'.

In spite of its considerable achievements there have been criticisms of the government's industrial policy. It has been argued that much of the investment has been in industries – like man-made fibres – which are capital intensive and which cannot therefore make much of an impact on the large pool of unemployment left by the old and declining industries. There have also been accusations that too many factories have been put up in the east – in areas where Protestants are in the majority. But three-quarters of the labour force is concentrated within 25 miles of Belfast – in the area where Protestants are in the majority. Although government inducements have been tailored to give the maximum incentive to industrialists to establish factories farther from Belfast, the labour catchment areas of communities in the west are often too small to support large factories – though the problem is now being tackled by a special Local Employment Development Unit.

Unemployment has however been consistently much higher in the predominantly Catholic areas of Northern Ireland and amongst unskilled workers – where Catholics are also in a majority – and both these things have not unnaturally fed the fires of the minority's resentment. It also seems beyond doubt that there has been discrimination on religious grounds by both Protestant and Catholic employers, based on the strong feeling in both communities that 'a man should look after his own' (– and since there are more Protestant employers than Catholic, this has undoubtedly had an influence on the higher percentage of unemployment in the Catholic community). This feeling has sometimes been expressed in terms which suggest that economic discrimination is an integral part of Unionist party policy. 'The Unionist party,' declared Robert Babington in 1949, 'should make it quite clear that it is loyalists who have the first choice of jobs. There is nothing wrong in this. Indeed, just the reverse; the Unionist party was founded to further the objects of the loyalists'. Perhaps the fairest conclusion would be that economic constraints have helped to justify Unionist policy, but that more could have been done for the economic development of areas where Catholics are in a majority.

When the Unionist opposition to Home Rule developed in the years before the first world war one of the main arguments for detaching Ulster had been that, since the North East was the only fully developed industrial area, an Ireland shorn of the six counties would not be economically viable and would therefore be unable to sustain its independence. Equally, when Griffith and Collins signed the Anglo-Irish treaty in 1921, they acquiesced in the partition of the country because they believed that the Boundary Commission promised by the Treaty would so diminish Northern Ireland that Northern Ireland in its turn would not be viable and would therefore be forced into reunion with the Free State. Until the war, both Northern Ireland and the Free State managed to keep afloat, but little more, and in that sense both sides were proved right. Since 1945 however, Northern Ireland has achieved greater prosperity than the Republic, but it is a prosperity founded on the economic aid she receives as an integral part of the United Kingdom; remove that assistance and the economy would collapse. Meanwhile, in the Republic, the 1960s have seen something of an economic miracle. Although the miracle has recently shown signs of being less miraculous than was at first thought (and although it has not been comprehensive enough to allow the Republic to establish a welfare state comparable to that established in the north) the Republic's economy is now probably the sounder of the two. But though it may be sounder, it is certainly not sound enough to keep the North in the style to which it has become accustomed. So both sides have been proved wrong – the Unionists, who didn't believe that the South could go it alone; and the Nationalists, who waited for the north to fall into their laps without calculating whether, if the bough ever broke, they would be able to hold the baby.

Some of the remarkable series of photographs taken of industry in the north in the years before the first world war – notably by R J Welch and W A Green (much of both their collections still survives). The first four are of the linen industry – yarn preparation, women operating jacquard looms, bleaching and the vast weaving shed at York Street Mills, Belfast.

These four photographs are of Harland and Wolff's yard – the workers leaving the yard (with the unfinished Titanic *in the background) and the engine works (left); on this page, a closer view of the* Olympic *under construction and the* Titanic *leaving Belfast on her fateful maiden voyage in April 1912.*

THIS HANDFUL OF DREAMS

'Nationality is their first objective' wrote Thomas Davis of himself and his friends in his prospectus for the *Nation*; 'Nationality which will not only raise our people from their poverty by securing them the blessing of a domestic legislation, but inflame and pacify them with a lofty and heroic love of country – a Nationality of the spirit as well as the letter.' If the people were to regain their self-respect, they must be reminded that they were the heirs to an ancient civilisation. 'If we live influenced by wind and sun and tree', urged Davis, 'and not by the passions and deeds of the past, we are a thriftless and a hopeless people.' And one of the major components of this revived nationality was the Irish language. Irish should be 'cherished, taught and esteemed' for 'a people without a language is only half a nation. A nation should guard its language more than its territories – 'tis a sure barrier, and more important frontier than fortress or river'.

When Davis was writing, in the early 1840s, Irish was the language of perhaps 2 million of his countrymen. In the years that followed it shrank steadily into the southern and western corners of Ireland. There were several reasons for this – the wave of emigration that followed the famine included a number of Irish speakers; the National Schools, set up in the 1830s, taught in English, ignoring the 'literature, history, arts and traditions of the people'; but above all because English was the language of law and politics, business and trade, the way of getting a better job and the means of rising in the social scale. Irish, on the other hand, was the badge of ignorance and poverty. As O'Connell had said: 'Although the Irish language is connected with many recollections that twine around the hearts of Irishmen, yet the superior *utility* of the English tongue, as the medium of all modern communication, is so great, that I can witness without a sigh the gradual disuse of the Irish'. Many agreed with him. Even in the 1840s Davis had complained that 'the middle classes think it a sign of vulgarity to speak Irish'. Fifty years later Douglas Hyde found the same. Waiting for a train in Co. Sligo, he spoke Irish to a little girl. 'The

girl answered me in Irish until her brother came in', he recorded. 'Arrah, now, Mary, said he, with what was intended to be a most bitter sneer, and isn't that a credit to you! And poor Mary – whom I had with difficulty persuaded to begin – immediately hung her head and changed to English.' The result of all this was that whereas, according to the census of 1851, $1\frac{1}{2}$ million people – 23 per cent of the population – spoke Irish, and more than 300,000 people spoke *only* Irish, the 1891 census found that the number of those able to speak Irish had fallen to 680,000, and only 38,000 spoke Irish alone.

During the same period, however, a number of scholars worked busily at the recovery and editing of ancient Irish texts. There was a long tradition – especially among Anglo-Irish Protestant gentlemen – of such scholarship, and during the nineteenth century more and more evidence began to accumulate of Ireland's rich and splendid past. It was on these solid foundations that the Gaelic League was able to build.

The Gaelic League, established in 1893 by Douglas Hyde, Eoin MacNeill and Father Eugene O'Growney, was dedicated to 'the preservation of Irish as the national language and the extension of its use as a spoken tongue'. It grew steadily, and though its activities were largely confined to the towns, by 1906 it had 100,000 members in 900 branches. The League also had considerable success in penetrating the formal educational system. In 1900 only 104 schools taught Irish; by 1906 this had risen to 3,000 – about a quarter of the total. In 1912, Hyde was instrumental in making Irish a compulsory subject for matriculation at the National University – which led to a steep increase in the number of students learning Irish in secondary schools. And, as a French observer noted in 1908, the enthusiasm of the League's members – 'young and old, clerks and artisans for the most part' for learning the language 'was serious, deep and infectious. Evidently, here are people who have been transformed to the core of their being by this somewhat severe study and by the importance of the role which they wish to play'. For many of those people to speak Irish for the first time was to have a real feeling of nationality.

The Gaelic League remained a minority movement, but although it was a minority movement, the minority that it reached was the minority which was eventually to win Irish independence. The young men who came to the front in Sinn Fein, and even in the IRB, in the years before 1916, had almost all come into politics through the Gaelic League – 'the most revolutionary influence that has ever come into Ireland' as Pearse said in 1914.

The League had been intended – as Davis had intended the national revival to be – non-political and non-sectarian. 'We cannot turn our back,' wrote Hyde, 'on the Davis ideal of every person in Ireland being an Irishman, no matter what their blood and politics'. But for many people the language revival was not an end in itself – the recapture of a lost culture. It was, as Griffith said, the means to an end; the fashioning of a new weapon in the constant struggle for national independence – a new weapon, because the old weapon, constitutional reform, seemed to have been buried with Parnell in his grave. Indeed, D. P. Moran, the editor of the separatist weekly *The Leader*, declared that every one of Ireland's political leaders, from Grattan to Parnell, whilst they professed to fight for Irish nationality, had only succeeded in throwing over Irish civilisation. 'The League found Ireland wrangling over the corpse of Parnell' wrote Moran. 'Under the inspiration of the new gospel of the Gaelic League the common man, much to his surprise, was driven to the conclusion that A and B were after all a pair of ordinary, unmannerly politicians and nothing else. And then the light dawned upon him that Politics is not Nationality and that the nineteenth century had been for Ireland mostly a century of humbug. That, in brief, is the revolution that the Gaelic League has worked, and that revolution has fundamentally altered the Irish problem.' Nationality, said Moran, was not politics, but civilisation. Ireland, he wrote, 'will never accomplish anything worthy of herself until she falls back upon her own language and traditions, and recovering there her old pride, self-respect and initia-

tive, develops and marches forward from thence'. It was impossible for the language revival to remain politically neutral, because it arose from a condition of inferiority, and was aimed at removing that inferiority. The Gaelic League, it has been rightly said, 'was not alone the rediscovery of the language, but a rediscovery of the nation'. A separate and distinct Irish culture was now seen as an indispensable element in any really meaningful independence.

But it was not just a separate and distinct *Irish* culture, it was also an overwhelmingly Catholic culture, accepting almost without question Catholic values and Catholic attitudes to life. The Roman Catholic church supported the movement,[1] as it had supported the Gaelic Athletic Association, because English literature was the product of a Protestant culture, and was therefore to be feared and opposed for its anti-Catholic and anti-religious tendencies. And from this it was easy to move on to a second proposition – that Irish rural life was the ideal ordering of society, that the peasant was God's Irishman, and that any criticism of this idyllic situation was sinister and subversive. In 1890, the Catholic *Lyceum*, reviewing Gavan Duffy's life of Thomas Davis, declared: 'While our peasants say their beads, and meditate on the mysteries of the Rosary, they can never come wholly under the sway of the doctrine that men were sent into the world to be happy and to make money. . . . He [Davis] saw in the factory system a monster that destroyed this ideal life, and he was its foe. He would have Ireland a nation of peasant owners.'

In fact, much of the Irish Ireland movement was concerned, in the end, with the rejection of the modern world. And, since England was the supreme example of success in the modern world, to reject England was not only politically satisfying, but morally satisfying as well. 'The ideal of the one race is beauty', wrote the *Irish Review* in 1912, 'whether in the mould of life or the spirit of action; the ideal of the other is power. There

---

[1] Though not at first – the bishops for example opposed compulsory Irish for admission to the National University.

Six of the major figures in the Anglo-Irish literary movement in the early years of this century. Left to right: Lady Gregory, Edward Martyn, George Moore, W B Yeats, J M Synge and AE (George Russell).

is only one kind of power that does not destroy beauty, and that is spiritual power – that the Celts once possessed and on that was their Empire founded.' Or as Pearse declared: 'The Gael is not like other men; the spade and the loom and the sword are not for him. But a destiny more glorious than that of Rome, more glorious than that of Britain awaits him: to become the saviour of idealism in modern intellectual and social life, the regenerator and rejuvenator of the literature of the world, the instructor of nations, the preacher of the gospel of nature – worship, hero-worship, God worship – such, Mr Chairman, is the destiny of the Gael.'

It would be easy, though wrong, to dismiss all this as conscious hypocrisy. However romantic and however illusory, the belief in the innate superiority of the Gaelic, Catholic and rural ideal was strongly held, and profoundly influenced the future development of Irish society.

And yet the greatest Irish literature of this period – the years between the death of Parnell in 1891 and the outbreak of the Great War in 1914 – this literature was not in Irish at all. It was in English, and it was the work of a small, intimate group with roots in the west of Ireland – Lady Gregory and Edward Martyn lived within a few miles of each other in Co. Galway; George Moore (though he was an absentee landlord) owned property in Co. Mayo; W. B. Yeats had been brought up in Co. Sligo; even J. M. Synge, who came from Co. Wicklow, drew his earliest inspiration from the Aran Islands off the west coast. Only AE (George Russell) who came from the north, was outside this western circle; only AE and Yeats were not members of the landed gentry, and only Martyn was a Catholic (Moore had lapsed very early in life). More than that, they were all members of that able and articulate minority which included men like Captain John Shawe-Taylor, Lady Gregory's nephew, who opened the way for the Wyndham Act of 1903, and Sir Horace Plunkett, the pioneer of the agricultural co-operative movement. Though they were all members of the Ascendancy, they made a deliberate attempt to cross

the traditional barriers of religion and politics, and to work for a united Irish nation with a genuine Irish culture. Even the Gaelic League was seen at first as part of the reconciliation process.[2]

There were several reasons for the emergence of such a group at this time. In the first place, to the perceptive eye, the old carefree days of the Anglo-Irish Ascendancy were rapidly coming to an end. The decline had begun with the Disestablishment of the Church of Ireland in 1869[3], and the growth of land purchase – culminating in the Wyndham Act of 1903 – destroyed the foundation of the landlords' power. The ordinary unthinking landlord followed his usual social round as blithely as ever, but to the intelligent few the writing was already on the wall. As the novelist Edith Somerville wrote: 'At Mount Music, where once the milk and honey had flowed with effortless abundance, each year brought increased stress. The rents grew less, the expense greater; that large and omnivorous item known as "keeping up the place" was as exacting as ever, the minor problems of household existence more acute. . . . Alien influences had poisoned the wells of friendship. Such rents as were paid were exacted by the hard hand of the law, and the tenants held indignation meetings against the landlord who refused to resign to them what they believed to be theirs and he was equally convinced was his'.

But the decline of the Ascendancy is not in itself a sufficient explanation of why its more perceptive members should have wished to come to terms with the 'other side'. Parnell's death and the continuing split in the parliamentary party seemed to have taken politics out of Irish life for a generation. Although this was not in fact the case – politics had simply taken a a different direction – the fact that this *appeared* to have happened made it easier to believe in a community of interests and in the possibility of fruitful co-operation in creating a common Irish culture.

This culture – 'that great Celtic phantasmagoria

[2] Douglas Hyde was, after all, the son of a Church of Ireland rector in Co. Roscommon.
[3] For the significance of Disestablishment, see chapter 10 (pp. 122–129).

whose meaning no man has discovered, nor any angel revealed', as Yeats called it – had been re-discovered first through the work of the mid-nineteenth century scholars, and through the popularisation of their work by Standish O'Grady[4] in the 1880s, and secondly by the publication in English (also in the 1880s) of fairy tales and folklore by Douglas Hyde. It was, said Yeats, the coming of a new power into literature, and he himself published two collections of folk-tales, describing one as 'this handful of dreams'. But it was not until Yeats met Lady Gregory in 1896 and began to stay regularly at her house, Coole Park, that the new movement, to create a literature in the English language out of Irish experience, really began to take shape.

There followed a body of achievement remarkable not only for its quality, but also for the speed and intensity with which the work was done. It included the creation of the Abbey Theatre by Yeats, Lady Gregory and Edward Martyn, Synge's plays and some of the best of Yeats's poetry. It was a literature based on an enthusiasm for the Irish past and the Irish countryside. 'The Greeks', wrote Yeats, 'the only perfect artists of the world, looked within their own borders, and we, like them, have legends which surpass, as I think, all legends but theirs in wild beauty; and in our land, as in theirs, there is no river or mountain that is not associated in the memory with some event or legend.' Ireland was a strange and beautiful land, wrote AE, 'and never a poet has lain on our hillsides but gentle, stately figures, with hearts shining like the sun, move through his dreams, over radiant grasses, in an enchanted world of their own; and it has become alive through every haunted rath and wood and mountain and lake, so that we can hardly think of it otherwise than as the shadow of the thought of God'. And the Anglo-Irish shared the romanticism of the Gaelic League about the Irish peasant. 'In Ireland alone among the nations that I know', wrote Yeats, 'you will find, away on the western seaboard, under broken roofs, a race of gentle-

men keep alive the ideals of a great time when man sang the heroic life with drawn swords in their hands'.

But a literature which was based on the Irish countryside and which constantly recalled the Irish past could not help having political overtones. The Gaelic revival had become identified with the revival of Irish national aspirations. Its supporters wanted a literature and a nation of their own: 'a new Irish civilisation quite distinct from the English'. A literature produced by Anglo-Irish writers, in English, was suspect because it was produced by a group who were by definition hostile to these aspirations.

And however enthusiastic they might be about the beauties of the Irish countryside and the magic of the Irish past, and however great their literary achievements, Yeats and his circle were still representatives of the Anglo-Irish ascendancy. Because of their history, their education and their environment, they were obviously much less nationally committed than the great body of their fellow countrymen. Yeats indeed had insisted from an early stage in his career that patriotism was 'an impure desire in an artist', and that literature must not be reduced to the status of propaganda; 'It seemed,' he complained, 'as if our new generation could not do its work unless we overcame the habit of making every Irish book, or poem, shoulder some political idea'. Thomas Davis and Young Ireland were responsible; they 'had sought a nation unified by political doctrine alone, a subservient art and letters aiding and abetting'. The result was that: 'All the past had been turned into a melodrama with Ireland for blameless hero'. And his friend, John Eglinton, hoped that he might live to see the day 'of what might be called, without any disrespect to Davis, the de-Davisisation of Irish national literature, that is to say, the getting rid of the notion that in Ireland a writer is to think first and foremost of interpreting the nationality of his country, and not simply of the burden which he was to deliver'. 'Literature,' he went on, 'must be as free as the elements; if that is to be cosmopolitan, it must be cosmopolitan.' But to committed nationalists 'cosmopolitanism' was doubly suspect; it was

[4] Who, in spite of his enthusiasm for Gaelic Ireland, was a staunch Unionist.

anti-national, and it was anti-Catholic. Indeed the group began to encounter a growing body of opposition which was based on the proposition that nothing could be tolerated which reflected either on the purity of Ireland's Catholicism, or on the integrity of Ireland's nationalism.

Nowhere was the opposition more vocal than amongst the audiences at the Abbey Theatre. In 1899, Yeats's play *The Countess Cathleen* was bitterly attacked as blasphemous and unpatriotic, because the Countess was prepared to sell her soul to the Devil to save her starving people from selling theirs. In 1903 Synge's play *In the Shadow of the Glen* – in which the heroine elopes with a tramp – was denounced by Arthur Griffith because 'all of us know that Irish women are the most virtuous in the world'. But the most famous episode was the riot that took place in 1907 at the first night of Synge's *The Playboy of the Western World* – a piece of earthy realism about life in Co. Mayo. The play was accused of lack of patriotism, lack of respect for women and actual blasphemy, but the uproar was caused by the line: 'It's Peegeen I'm seeking only and what'd I care if you brought me a drift of chosen females standing in their shifts itself' – 'a word,' said one shocked observer, 'that no refined woman would mention, even to herself'. Such reactions were due as much as anything to the extreme sensitivity of nationalist feeling – a feeling which was all the more powerful because it sprang from a deep, but largely unconscious, sense of inferiority. And, as this nationalist feeling became more self-confident, it also grew increasingly aggressive, narrow-minded and intolerant. It represented in fact the perfected fruit of centuries of subordination. What made the nationalist opposition to the Anglo-Irish literary revival so formidable was that the very Ascendancy which had exacted this subordination for so long was now visibly breaking up, so that nationalist and Catholic distaste for the style and philosophy of the revival was united with a contempt for the tradition from which the Anglo-Irish sprang, a contempt which was now reinforced by a realisation that the tradition itself was approaching its end. 'How could a literary movement be in any sense national', wrote John Eglinton later, 'when the interest of the whole nation lay in extirpating the conditions which produced it.'

Because the Gaelic revival became such a powerful weapon in the struggle for national independence, nationalists rejected the Anglo-Irish attempt to come to terms with Gaelic culture. For the same reason, when an independent Irish state was finally established in 1922, it took its character from the ideals of those who had fought for it. Prominent among those ideals was the conviction that the Irish language was an essential element in the establishment of a separate national identity – 'Ireland not free merely, but Gaelic as well', as Patrick Pearse had said.

The constitution of the Irish Republic declares that 'the Irish language is the first official language'; a recent government White Paper adds 'the Irish language is the most distinctive sign of our nationality. Our present position as an independent State derives in large measure from the idealism evoked by the Irish language movement', and 'the national aim is to restore the Irish language as a general medium of communication'. This aim is immediately visible to the visitor in the use of the language in street signs, public notices, on pillar boxes, telephone booths and post offices, public lavatories, destination signs on buses, and so on. But this is only the surface manifestation of the official determination to 'cherish and develop the Irish language as an effective, continuing expression of our separate identity'.

There have been two major instruments in the attempt to revive the Irish language since 1922 – those parts of the country (small in 1922, and even smaller in 1974) where Irish is still widely spoken: the Gaeltacht; and the schools. The determination of the new State to put the principles of its founders into practice was demonstrated in one of the earliest pronouncements of the Free State government – that Irish should be taught, or used as the medium of instruction, in all primary schools for at least an hour a day. In 1926 a second national education programme was launched, aimed at 'the strengthening of the national fibre by giving the language, history, music and traditions of Ireland their natural place in the life of Irish schools'. 'When a teacher is competent to teach through Irish and where children can assimilate the instruction so given', said the Department of Education, 'the teacher should endeavour to extend the use of Irish as a medium of instruction as far as possible.' In practice this meant that all infant classes were taught in Irish, that the time spent on teaching other subjects in primary schools was reduced to allow more time for teaching Irish, and that in many schools *all* subjects were taught in Irish.

But in spite of a vigorous programme designed to increase the number of teachers qualified to teach 'through the medium' of Irish, not enough teachers knew Irish well enough to ensure the programme's success. There were not enough textbooks either, and many of these were unsuitable – 97,000 copies of 68 such textbooks had to be burned in 1968. In 1941 the Irish National Teachers Organisation reported that the programme was causing children much unnecessary suffering without any worthwhile educational return – especially in subjects like mathematics. Although the regulations were relaxed in the late 1940s a minority report of the Council of Education in 1951 reported widespread 'apathy, resentment, passive resistance and actual hostility' to the language.

For many, Irish has undoubtedly continued to mean 'a dull, dreary round of memory tests and monotonous repetitions that kill all interest and initiative'. This has been a significant factor in conditioning parents' attitudes to Irish teaching, which has in turn had a considerable influence on their children's attitude to the language. This has been reinforced by the fact that until 1968 those who failed Irish in their school leaving examinations failed the whole examination,[5] and that not until 1973 did Irish cease to be a compulsory subject in that examination. Nevertheless a majority would probably still subscribe – at least in principle – to the recent official statement that 'no Irish child can be regarded as fully educated if he grows up without a knowledge of the Irish language and that the educational system will be seriously defective if it does not provide for the teaching of Irish to all children'.

Certainly a large number of people in the Irish Republic now understand Irish – over 700,000 of them are classified as Irish-speaking in the 1961 census, though few speak the language with real ease. Irish is compulsory for entry into, and promotion within, the Civil Service and for many of the professions, but in 1959 only 14 per cent of all civil servants spoke the language fluently, and only 2 per cent of government business was actually conducted in Irish. Even in the Dail, few speeches, even in debates on the Irish language, are ever made in Irish. The problem is that the vast majority of the population already speak English and have no incentive to speak Irish. As the Commission on the Restoration of the Irish Language reported in 1963: 'The majority of Irish youth have not attained a ready command of the language by the time they leave school; among those who have attained it, many soon lose it for want of contact with the language in after life; and of those who retain it, many are shy about using the language except in chosen company, lest they may offend or call attention to themselves or be ridiculed'.

Indeed there are a dwindling number who speak Irish as their first language. There were 257,000 in 1926,[6] but there are probably only about 30,000 today, and none who speak only Irish – and, largely because of this, the Irish spoken today has neither the fluency, the precision or the vigour that it had fifty years ago. These Irish speakers are concentrated in the Gaeltacht – a few small areas mainly on the west coast. Because these areas are amongst those which are economically the least viable, emigration has been very heavy. Their population – which was 245,000 in 1926 – has steadily declined, and though it has been falling less fast in the

[5] Very few actually failed, though the psychological effect was probably more significant than the numbers suggest.

[6] This is the figure given in the 1926 census; it probably overstates the numbers who genuinely spoke Irish as their first language.

The Gaeltacht, as defined in 1956. The seven areas, with their population in 1966, are: 1 Donegal (23,932) 2 Mayo (14,762) 3 Galway (21,716) 4 Kerry (8,095) 5 Cork (3,368) 6 Waterford (833) and 7 Meath (924). Meath was the only area to increase in population between 1961 and 1966. The only town in all seven areas with a population of more than a thousand is Dingle in Co Kerry, and only three others have a population of more than 500.

of Ireland'. The aim of Government policy therefore is 'to encourage and expand suitable economic activities and to improve social conditions so that those residing there, who use the Irish language as their normal medium of communication, will have adequate opportunities of securing gainful employment and of enjoying reasonable living standards'.

Although a government commission recommended as long ago as 1926 that a wide ranging programme of government assistance should be undertaken to halt the Gaeltacht's decline, it was not until 1956 that a separate government department was set up to look after these areas, and not until 1958 that Gaeltarra Eireann was established to co-ordinate government aid. And although this has been considerable – £4 million a year is currently being spent on development in the Gaeltacht – too little may still have been given too late. Only about 7,700 people are employed in industry (and many, once trained by Gaeltarra Eireann, have left the Gaeltacht). Two-thirds of the Gaeltacht's population are still farmers; two-thirds of them own farms with less than 40 acres of land, and two-thirds of them are over 50, with no prospective heirs.

But the government is in a difficult dilema. If it encourages people to stay in the Gaeltacht by developing industry and tourism, then the special character of the Gaeltacht may be destroyed. If, on the other hand, it does nothing, the language may die out altogether. This may still not happen. If it does however it will not be because of the mistakes of an over-ambitious educational policy, or because of an insufficiently vigorous attack on the social and economic problems of the Gaeltacht. A more important reason for the failure of an Irish-speaking State to emerge in the fifty years since 1922 has been the very strength of its founders' belief in such a state. 'We only succeeded after we had begun to get back to our Irish ways' said Collins. 'We can only keep out the enemy and all other enemies by completing that task.' The identification of the language with the struggle for independence, as a recent historian has said, has made 'rational appraisal impossible and rational solutions politically inexpedi-

last 15 years, it had fallen by 1971 to a little over 70,000 The preservation and strengthening of the Gaeltacht is therefore essential to any programme for the restoration of the Irish language. 'Whatever further steps towards the restoration of the language might be postponed to future generations', wrote the 1963 Commission, 'the saving of the Gaeltacht cannot be deferred. If this generation fails to save it, there will be no Gaeltacht left for the next generation to save.' But on the other hand the preservation and strengthening of the Gaeltacht 'must not be approached as if it were an attempt to preserve in one corner of the country an aboriginal reservation to remind us of the past; it can be successful only as part of the movement to preserve the Irish language and spread it as the normal language ent'. Any opposition to the language, however mildly expressed, or rationally based, has been denounced as anti-national.[7] Many people – notably politicians – have also continued to pay lip service to the ideal without really believing in it, and as a result, in the words of a recent government report on development in the Gaeltacht 'many people see Irish as associated with negative values which turn them away from, rather than towards it' – values like compulsion, intolerance, hypocrisy and xenophobia.

Some of the values which a lukewarm public regards as negative however, are central to the philosophy of the Gaelic revival. For the Gaelic revival was not just a movement to revive the Irish language and Irish culture; it was a movement which idealised the traditional way of life and the traditional values of the rural society which had preserved that language and that culture. This dedication to traditional values was well expressed by President De Valera in a radio broadcast in 1943: 'The Ireland that we dreamed of would be the home of the people who valued material wealth only as a basis for right living; of a people who, satisfied with frugal comfort, devoted their leisure to the things of the spirit; a land whose countryside would be bright with cosy homesteads, whose fields and villages would be joyous with the sounds of industry, with the romping of sturdy children, the contests of athletic youth and the laughter of happy maidens, whose firesides would be forums for the wisdom of serene old age.' But De Valera's vision was not shared by a majority of people, who have continued to identify the Irish language not with frugal comfort and right living, but with poverty and backwardness, and who have consequently left the countryside in their thousands for the modern, urban, sophisticated and enlightened world they associate with English.

But they have by no means abandoned Irish culture altogether. The Gaelic Athletic Association has more than 3,000 clubs; hurling and Gaelic football continue to attract large crowds, and there are more than 70,000 supporters at Croke Park in Dublin for the all-Ireland championships. The fleadhs (festivals) organised by the Traditional Music Society of Ireland are very popular; the all-Ireland fleadh may attract up to 100,000 people. And Gael Linn, founded in 1953 by a group of young radicals in the Gaelic League, has made a determined attempt to get Irish culture to a wider public – through plays, films, records, cabaret – even bingo, with the numbers called in Irish.

The fact remains that, in the government's words, 'the widespread but often passive public sentiment in favour of the language' has not been transformed into a 'willingness to make a sustained personal effort to achieve the national aim'. At Easter 1966 De Valera declared that without the language Ireland 'would sink into an amorphous cosmopolitanism – without a past, or a distinguishable future. To avoid such a fate, we of this generation must see that our language lives. That would be the resolve of the men and women of 1916. Will it not be the resolve of the young men and women of 1966?'

The people of Ireland would like to avoid that fate. Even if they have the resolve, however, it remains an open question whether they will be able to do so.

[7] Though many people in the Republic have always thought of the Irish language as having great potential for encouraging national unity, this connection has been the main reason why the Irish language continues to be regarded with considerable suspicion by Unionists in Northern Ireland.

HOME RULE IS ROME RULE

'We are the Established Church,' wrote Richard Chenevix Trench, the Anglican Archbishop of Dublin in 1865, 'because we are the Church which the State believes to be true.' For more than three hundred years the church in Ireland had meant the Church of Ireland. Like the Church of England, the Anglican church of Ireland was part of the establishment, and in Ireland that had meant that it was an integral part of the Protestant Ascendancy, the church of wealth, status and influence, a rich and powerful minority with a special position. This special position was acknowledged by the Act of Union in 1800, which united the established Churches of England and Ireland and declared that 'the continuation and preservation of the said United Church as the established church of England and Ireland shall be deemed and taken to be an essential and fundamental part of the Union'.

And yet, since the passing of the Act of Union, the Church of Ireland has been almost continuously in retreat. The tithe[1] wars of the 1830s weakened the economic position of the clergy. Gladstone's Irish Church Act of 1869 disestablished and disendowed the Church of Ireland.[2] The assumption behind the Act – in the words of the Catholic Archbishop of Dublin, Paul Cullen – was that 'peace and love for authority can never be established in Ireland as long as the Catholics shall be obliged to support a Protestant establishment and to submit to a Protestant Ascendancy'; and though the Church of Ireland retained much of its wealth after 1869, Disestablishment destroyed its privileged position. During the next forty years land reform removed the support of the old governing class. And finally the Anglo-Irish war and the partition of the country deprived the Church of the shield of British protection. Today its members are a tiny minority (now about 5 per cent) of the population of the Republic, and a large – but by no means dominant – group in Northern Ireland (where members of the Church of Ireland now form about a quarter of the population).

Whereas the Church of Ireland in the south has remained the church of a comfortable and influential minority, a self-sufficient group whose position has, on the whole, been respected by the State, in the north on the other hand – though it has remained the church of the landed gentry – the Church of Ireland's main strength is in urban areas. This curious combination of a denomination heavily represented at the two ends of the social scale has had important consequences for the political history of Ulster Unionism.

When we speak of the church in Ireland today we usually mean the Roman Catholic Church, the church to which 95 per cent of the Republic's population and about one third of the population of Northern Ireland now belong, the church (as one nationalist historian has written) 'of the people, from the people, and in the main with the people'. In fact the identity of interest between church and people has been nothing like as close as either the church or nationalist historians would like us to believe. In particular the Roman Catholic Church has consistently opposed revolutionary violence, denouncing the Fenians from the pulpit, and excommunicating the Irregulars during the Civil War. It also took a major part in the attack on Parnell after the O'Shea divorce case and the split in the Nationalist party in 1891.

On the other hand, at the beginning of the nineteenth century the Catholic population 'had few persons of education, except the priests, to lead or to stand by them on the political vantage ground which they had newly obtained', and it was not surprising, therefore, as one apologist wrote in 1906, that 'from the early days of the O'Connell movement, when the Irish priest first appeared on the public platform after the penal times, his action in Irish public affairs has been, down to the present day, chiefly political'. The Roman Catholic clergy had been closely involved both in the struggle for Catholic Emancipation in the 1820s, and in the Repeal Campaign of the 1840s. In the same way they took a leading part both in the agitation for land reform

---

[1] Tithe was a tax levied by, and payable to, all clergymen of the established church; in 1838 it was converted into a fixed charge and responsibility for payment transferred from tenants to landlords.

[2] That is, the legal connection between church and state was broken, and all church property put in the hands of 'Commissioners for Irish church temporalities'.

and in the Home Rule movement during the 1880s; in February 1886 the Bishops declared that it was their 'firm and conscientious conviction' that only Home Rule could satisfy 'the legitimate aspirations of the Irish people'.

Many Protestants however, especially in the north, had a deep-rooted suspicion of Rome, 'the executors of the decrees of Pope Satan and his cardinals below', which they believed to be ever on the watch 'to overthrow the work of the Reformation in these islands'. This suspicion was strengthened by the declaration of Papal infallibility at the first Vatican Council in 1870, denounced by the 1878 Lambeth Conference as 'an invasion of the attributes of Our Lord Jesus Christ'. They also had vivid folk memories of past persecutions – especially in 1641 and 1798. As the Rev. William Corkey declared in 1912: 'The people of Ulster are the descendants of men who bore a brave and manly part in the fierce struggle on behalf of civil and religious liberty' (a reference, of course, to the events of 1689-90). 'The story of the bitter experience endured under the Church of Rome has been handed down from generation to generation. There is scarcely a home in Ulster that cannot tell the story of how some member suffered for the Truth of God. You cannot blot the history of the past out of the memory of the Evangelical Christians of Ulster.'

The Protestant minority feared that the influence of the Roman Catholic clergy in politics, and the influence which they believed was exerted by the Papacy on the Roman Catholic clergy, would together mean that in an independent Ireland the influence of the Roman Catholic Church would be overwhelming – that Home Rule would mean Rome Rule. This fear was a major factor in the resistance to Home Rule before 1914. As the Rev. J. O. Hannay wrote, in a pamphlet called *Home Rule Problems* in 1911, many Unionists 'think it highly probable that in an independent or semi-independent Ireland, where Roman Catholics would be in a majority of three to one, Protestants would suffer all sorts of unpleasantness. Phrases of the most picturesque violence are used freely, and we are asked to contemplate the possibility of our Roman Catholic fellow-countrymen gorging themselves upon the blood and treasure of Irish Protestants'.

The fear of Rome was not based entirely on fantasy. In August 1908, for example, Pope Pius X promulgated the Decree *Ne Temere* which laid down that no marriage between a Roman Catholic and a Protestant which had not been celebrated according to the rites of the Roman Catholic church could be regarded as valid. In 1908, a Mrs McCann, who had married her Roman Catholic husband in a Presbyterian church in Belfast, refused to be re-married by a Roman Catholic priest. As a result, she was – according to the minutes of the General Assembly of the Presbyterian church – 'deserted by her husband, deprived of her children and her household effects, and left homeless and penniless on the streets of Belfast.' It seems clear that this was a powerful argument in the campaign against Home Rule. 'Is it any wonder that we in Ulster refuse to come under Rome?', demanded the Rev. William Corkey, at the annual meeting of the Evangelical Alliance in May 1912, 'and when Mr Redmond and Mr Devlin make love to the Protestants of the North and say "Come unto our arms and we will be kind and good to you" is it any wonder that Ulster, like a fair young bride, stands aghast and says, "I will never consent to a mixed marriage, for I know how your Church always treats the Protestant partner?" And until Rome learns to treat the Protestant fairly, Ulster will never consent to be married to the rest of Ireland'.

It was not surprising, therefore, that when northern Protestants had secured their ascendancy in a separate Northern Ireland they were determined that Catholics should not threaten their position. 'It has been a spiritual combat between the powers of darkness represented by the besieging force and the Lord of Hosts represented by the Protestants within the walls', said the preacher at an Apprentice Boys of Londonderry service in August 1936; 'the contest which the original Apprentice Boys waged is still going on. Ulstermen still represent the same traditions for which the men of Derry stood during the siege'. It was not surprising either that the relationship between church and state in the south should have been scrutinised so constantly and so vigilantly since partition for evidence that Home Rule continued to mean Rome Rule. To many Protestants in the north such evidence is overwhelming.

They find it first in what they see as the sectarian clauses of the Republic's constitution, which (until that article was repealed in December 1972) recognised 'the special position of the Holy Catholic Apostolic and Roman church as the guardian of the Faith professed by the great majority of the citizens'. The Republic's constitution still incorporates Roman Catholic social teaching in the sections dealing with the family, notably in the clause stating that 'no Law shall be enacted providing for the grant of a dissolution of marriage'. They find it also in legislation, especially in the Criminal Law Amendment Act of 1935 which forbids the sale of contraceptives – their advertisement is also banned by the Censorship of Publications Acts of 1929 and 1946. The Censorship Acts have also, until very recently, kept the works of a number of the world's greatest writers out of Ireland. Though, since 1967, some of the more eccentric prohibitions have been removed, the population of the Irish Republic is still denied a free choice either of what it may read or of what films it may see (films have also been censored by law since 1923). Such legislation has received the unequivocal support of the Roman Catholic Church – 'The one who desires to limit the number of his children will come under God's anger'; 'No power on earth can break the marriage bond until death'; 'As for the rights of art and literature, neither has any rights against God'.

But it is not just the condemnation of contraception and divorce, or the support for censorship on *moral* grounds which has offended and alarmed Protestants (many of whom were probably as conservative in their views on these matters as Catholics); it was the assumption that the Catholic religion is the true religion and that Protestants have no natural right to practice a false one. Although few would now agree with the claim made in the 1930s by the Catholic Archbishop of Armagh, Cardinal Joseph MacRory, that Protestants were 'not even a part of the church of Christ' – and none would now dare to say so in public – the assumption that the Catholic religion is the true religion still conditions Catholic attitudes. Nowhere has this been more apparent than in the question of mixed marriages, perhaps the most divisive of all issues between Protestants and Catholics in Ireland. The regulations adopted by the Irish hierarchy, which describe the obligation to bring up the children of a mixed marriage as Catholics as a matter of Divine Law, are much more rigid than the regulations of the hierarchies in most other countries. In 1961 something like a third of all Protestant men and a fifth of all Protestant women in the Republic married Catholics, and many Protestants would argue that the strictness with which the Catholic regulations on mixed marriages are interpreted has contributed more than anything else to the decline of the Protestant population in the Republic in the past fifty years (327,000 in 1911, 221,000 in 1926 and 130,000 today) – and could lead to its virtual extinction in the foreseeable future. For that reason, as Dr Kenneth Milne said recently: 'It is the great obstacle that exists to the integration of Catholic and Protestant society in Ireland, whatever it may achieve in terms of unconditional surrender'.

But it is the power of the hierarchy that the northern Irish Protestant fears most. Though this power is no longer as widespread nor as all-pervasive as some believe, the bishops have certainly had a considerable influence on a number of pieces of legislation in the South. The real question however is: when the hierarchy speaks out against the government, who backs down? Politicians have tended to regard the church as just another pressure group. 'I felt they were expressing their concern as citizens with certain things that were happening,' said Sean Lemass, in an interview published in 1969, 'but they never made any attempt to impose their views on me'. The bishops, on the other hand, have taken a more exalted view of their role. As Bishop Lucey of Cork said in 1955: 'When the bishops in this country took a stand not so long ago on the Health Bill, they were not acting as a mere pressure group; they were not exercising the democratic rights they undoubtedly had as citizens to make representation directly to the government. They intervened on the higher ground that the Church is the divinely appointed guardian and interpreter of the moral law. . . . In a word, their position was that they were the final arbiters of right and wrong even in political matters.'

This statement, though it was made by a bishop of the old school, and made nearly twenty years ago, is frequently cited in the north as proof of the fact that the Irish Republic is a theocratic state. In fact, however, the closeness of the connection between church and state has varied considerably, and to a certain extent according to which party has been in power – Fianna Fail having shown rather more readiness to stand up to the hierarchy than Fine Gael, though it has certainly not done so consistently.

Broadly speaking, up to about 1940 the hierarchy left its imprint very markedly on Irish public life. This was the period when divorce was prohibited, the sale of contraceptives banned, dance halls stringently regulated in an attempt to enforce chastity, and censorship imposed both on literature and the cinema. It was also the period when De Valera attempted to embody the country's essential Catholicism in its constitution. 'There are 93 per cent of the population in this part of Ireland and 75 per cent of the people of Ireland as a whole who belong to the Catholic Church, who believe in its teachings, and whose whole philosophy of life is the philosophy that comes from its teachings' he said during the debate on the 1937 constitution. 'If we are going to have a democratic state, if we are going to be ruled by the representatives of the people, it is clear that their whole philosophy of life is going to affect that, and that has to be borne in mind and the recognition of it is important.' At that point in time the tastes of the hierarchy and their flocks seem on the whole to have coincided. The strict discipline imposed by the Church may have driven young men and women from the joyless countryside – in Co. Kerry, for example,

curates set light to the dancing platforms at country cross-roads and at Clones, Co. Monaghan (only a few miles from the border with Northern Ireland) Canon Marron, the parish priest, insisted that men should sit on one side of the local cinema and women on the other. But so strong was the innate puritanism of the people and so ingrained was their readiness to bow to authority – especially divinely appointed authority – that there was virtually no protest.

This authoritarian, interventionist tendency of the church was, if anything, strengthened in the 1940s and 1950s. This was the period of 'integralism': the idea that Catholic doctrines on law, morality and social organisation should be intregrated as fully as possible into the fabric of the state. In the years after 1945, extensive social welfare legislation became necessary if Eire was to be kept even remotely in line with what was happening in the rest of the British Isles, and especially north of the border. The bishops' major preoccupation was with the sanctity of the family, and it was this which led first to difficulties with the Health Act of 1947, and then to the famous clash between church and state over Dr Noel Brownes' Mother and Child Health Services scheme.

In October 1950 Dr Browne's proposal for free voluntary medical services for mothers and all children under 16 was immediately attacked by the bishops. 'The right to provide for the health of children', they declared, 'belongs to parents, not the state. The state has the right to intervene only in a subordinate capacity; to supplement, not to supplant.' This, however, was not their only concern (and, given the extreme poverty of many large Catholic families, it would have been difficult for the hierarchy to sustain their case on these grounds alone). The bishops were also anxious that the education for motherhood envisaged in the scheme would include sex education: 'We regard with the greatest apprehension the proposal to give to local medical officers the right to tell Catholic girls and women how they should behave in regard to this sphere of conduct, at once so delicate and sacred.' As the crisis developed Dr Browne became steadily more isolated.

This was due partly to his own political inexperience (he had only entered the Dail in 1948 and immediately became Minister of Health), partly to the fact that the scheme alienated Irish doctors, who smelt the approach of socialism, and partly to a series of misunderstandings which led Browne to believe that he had placated the hierarchy, when in fact he had done nothing of the sort.

On 5 April 1951, the bishops repeated their opposition to the scheme: 'The Hierarchy cannot approve of any scheme which, in its general tendency, must foster undue control by the state in a sphere so delicate and so intimately concerned with morals' and must therefore regard the scheme proposed by the Minister of Health as 'opposed to Catholic social teaching'. As a result the government abandoned the scheme and Browne was forced to resign.

What struck outside observers so forcibly was not merely that the hierarchy had the power to destroy the scheme, but that the government should have given way so completely. As the Taoiseach, J. A. Costello, wrote to Browne: 'I have no doubt that all my colleagues, and in particular yourself, would not be party to any proposals affecting moral questions which would, or might come into, conflict with the definite teaching of the Catholic Church.' The *Irish Times* observed bitterly that 'the Roman Catholic Church would seem to be the effective government of this country', but Mr Costello unrepentantly defended himself in the Dail. 'I, as a Catholic, obey my Church authorities and will continue to do so, in spite of the *Irish Times* or anything else.' Even Dr Browne in his speech of resignation said: 'I, as a Catholic, accept unequivocally and unreservedly the views of the hierarchy on this matter'. Perhaps the most revealing comment of all however was Costello's claim that: 'All these matters could have been, and ought to have been, dealt with calmly, in quiet and in council, without the public becoming aware of the matter. The public never ought to have become aware of the matter'.

It is easy to imagine the effect of this affair in the north, especially as it came so soon after the verbal passage of arms between the two governments during the 1949 election in Northern Ireland and the formation of the all-party Anti-Partition Committee in Dublin. The Ulster Unionists immediately published a pamphlet claiming that the whole episode made it clear that 'in any matter where the Roman Catholic Church decides to intervene the Eire government must accept the Church's policy and decision irrespective of all other considerations'. Even today the Mother and Child scheme is cited in the north as an example of the kind of thing Protestants would have to put up with in a united Ireland. What is not admitted in the north, but seems nearer the truth, is that while the crisis was undoubtedly a particularly crass example of ecclesiastical dictation, it was a rare one even at the time and has never been repeated since.

Indeed, from the early 1960s onwards, the attitude of the hierarchy seems to have been much less rigid. This is partly the result of improved methods of ecclesiastical diplomacy, partly the realisation that social questions are more complex than they once appeared, and partly because of the change in the religious climate connected with the second Vatican Council. Though the then Archbishop of Dublin, John McQuaid, sought to reassure his flock on his return from Rome with the words: 'You may have been worried by much talk of changes to come. Allow me to reassure you. No change will worry the tranquility of your Christian lives' – the strength of the ecumenical movement could not be entirely ignored, even in Ireland. In recent years there has been a much greater willingness to abandon the church's special position, to involve the laity more in the affairs of the church and to allow freer discussion of controversial issues. But it would be wrong to over-estimate the liberalising tendencies within the Irish church; the forces of conservatism are still formidable. These forces have recently received added encouragement from the Papal edict on birth control, Humanae Vitae, which was a considerable setback for liberal Catholics.

It would be wrong however to consider Irish Catholicism simply in terms of church and state. Even today, the visitor to Ireland is struck by the fact that

Ireland is still visibly a Catholic country – by the massive church attendances, the religious literature on the bookstalls, the country shrines, the planeloads of pilgrims to Lourdes. There is also the respect for the cloth, for the traditional authority of the priest, who is still the natural (and in the countryside often the only) leader. Even in the towns the parish remains the social unit and the priest the most significant local figure – so much so that some priests now complain (to reverse the traditional phrase) that it is they who are people-ridden. All this creates a social atmosphere which is stronger than positive action in affecting the attitude of Protestants to life in a Catholic country. The Catholic atmosphere of life in the south has also inhibited the state's involvement in social welfare, with the result that care for the poor, the old, the mentally ill and the handicapped is generally insufficient, often old-fashioned and sometimes incompetently administered; and though this has changed a good deal in recent years, social welfare provisions in Northern Ireland remain markedly superior to those in the Republic.

This Catholic ethos has also affected the educational system. Primary schools almost invariably have clergy as their managers – with the power to appoint the teachers – and most secondary education is in the hands of religious orders. The church forbids parents to send children to non-Catholic schools, and – until 1970 – no Catholic was allowed to attend Trinity College, Dublin without episcopal permission 'under pain of grave sin'. Protestants, on the other hand, have found it increasingly difficult to send their children to Protestant schools, largely because of the high cost – especially at secondary level – of providing adequate education for such a scattered community.[3] More and more children are therefore being sent to Catholic schools. And for Catholics, education means Catholic education. As the guide for Catholic teachers, pub-

lished in 1952, says: 'The teacher must seek to Catholocise the classroom treatment of the subject, and to press out of it the fullest yield of intellectual support to the faith'.

During the last ten years however remarkable and extensive changes have been taking place in Irish society. Above all, there has been a growing acceptance of the need for change. This has been stimulated by greater prosperity, by increasing contacts with foreign tourists and foreign businessmen, and by the growing tendency of the Irish themselves to travel abroad; but above all perhaps by what they have seen on television, especially on the east coast where British television can be received as well. Television indeed has been a dramatic and compelling intrusion of the twentieth century into a conservative and conformist society; and this is certain to change the situation still more as time goes on. However swift and however radical such changes may be however, it will still take some time to convince many in the north of their reality.

This is partly because, whilst it is fair to describe the Republic of Ireland as a Catholic society, it would not be very misleading to describe Northern Ireland as a Presbyterian society. Since religious observance in Northern Ireland is a badge of political difference, it is not surprising that the figures for church attendance, baptisms and marriages are much higher for all the Protestant churches there than in the rest of the United Kingdom, and there are strong social pressures in the north, as in the south, to conform to the prevailing religious – in this case Protestant – ethos. But since both Protestant and Catholic in Northern Ireland are so conscious of their differences, it is not surprising that Protestants should seek to emphasise those aspects of their faith which differentiate them most strongly from Roman Catholics – and those aspects are characteristically Presbyterian.

The Presbyterian church has rather more members in the north than the Church of Ireland – 413,000 against 345,000 in 1961. It is also largely confined to Northern Ireland; it could lose its whole membership outside the six counties 'without any serious modi-

[3] Until 1967, only primary education was paid for directly by the state; but even now that secondary education is also subsidised, Protestant schools are at a disadvantage because their teachers (unlike many teachers in Catholic schools, who are in religious orders) have to be paid.

fication of its structure, or injury to its tradition'. The Church of Ireland, on the other hand, is an all-Ireland institution, and this is important both for its structure and its tradition. The Presbyterian church is a solid middle class church with a deep belief in the traditional Scots virtues of industry and thrift, hard work and honest dealing, a church whose members were traditionally 'raised on porridge and the shorter catechism'.

It was Presbyterianism which was mainly responsible for putting the stamp of Calvinistic piety on northern society; for the dour sabbatarianism – which still closes the pubs on Sundays and which used, until very recently, to frown on those who travelled by bus, or dug their gardens on the Sabbath; for the gloomy pre-occupation with death and hell, the puritanical obsession with sexual morality (one quality at least which many Irish Protestants share with many Irish Catholics); the fundamentalism of a religion based largely on the Old Testament and the Ten Commandments, and one given to statements like: 'It is not an easy road we are travelling to Heaven and God does not intend it to be easy'; 'We are born in sin and shapen in iniquity'; 'Remember, Hell is the inevitable alternative to Heaven'; 'The Bible is the law of God – to obey it is eternal life; to disobey it is eternal death'; 'If the Sabbath be forgotten, then the Gospel will cease to be preached'.

Presbyterianism is also responsible for the anti-Catholic and anti-Papal tone of Protestant feeling in the north. This is an intensely strong and deep sentiment – and one shared by many members of the Church of Ireland – though to many Presbyterians the Church of Ireland is itself suspect because of its hierarchichal structure, its supposed ritualistic tendencies and its residual sense of social superiority – 'although she would arrogate to herself exclusively the name *Protestant*, of all the churches of the Reformation she has the least right to it'. The Presbyterian Church's confession of faith refers to the Pope as Anti-Christ,[4] and many Presbyterians would agree with phrases like 'the mockery of the mass', 'the pagan idolatries of Romish worship', and 'the fraud of the papacy', to which the more radical preachers – another characteristic feature of the Presbyterian church – are much given. Many too would relish the words of Orange songs, like:

Scarlet Church of all uncleanness
Sink thou to the deep abyss,
To the orgies of obsceneness.
Where the hell-bound furies hiss;
Where thy father Satan's eye
May hail thee, blood-stained Papacy!

and:

Loud hail the Lodges, in triumph we'll sing
To our great Jehovah and Israel's king
Who kept us from worshipping idols of brass,
Or eating our Saviour when they go to the mass.

These feelings are not often so forcefully expressed, but they run deep. And there is a positive side to the extreme dislike and distrust of Rome. This is based partly on the feeling that Presbyterianism seeks to influence men's consciences, but that the Catholic church seeks to control men's minds, denying them direct and personal contact with God. It is also due partly to the fact that the structure of the Presbyterian church, from the Kirk Session through the Presbytery to the General Assembly, is very democratic, in strong contrast to the hierarchichal, authoritarian structure of the Catholic church. It is not surprising therefore, that the real 'ultra' in Northern Ireland, though he may be an Anglican, is more likely to be a Presbyterian. Although in its earliest days the Orange Order was connected more directly with the Anglican ascendancy, in recent years the organisation has become increasingly identified with Presbyterianism.

Neither the philosophy nor the structure of the Protestant churches lend themselves to quite the same relationship between church and state as in the south.

---

[4] It is only fair to point out however that the Westminster Confession is, or has been, shared by Presbyterians throughout the English-speaking world.

There has however been considerable friction in several places over the way in which the Catholic community spends its Sunday. In 1959, for example, the Unionist Council in Portadown refused to licence three Catholic church halls for dancing on Sundays – though an appeal against the decision was then upheld by the county court. The concerted opposition of the Protestant churches also prevented the operation of the sections of the 1923 Education Act which provided that there should be no religious instruction in maintained schools, and that teachers should not be appointed for their religious beliefs.[5]

As the Rev. William Corkey declared: 'We cannot be expected to view with equanimity the working of an Act which takes away from the Protestant Churches all association with education, and at the same time endows the Church of Rome and entrenches her clergy more firmly than ever in the educational system of our country'. The result was that the act was amended and in 1930 Lord Craigavon assured the Protestant churches that they should have: 'Firstly, security for the permanence of Bible teaching in all provided and transferred schools' (that is, all local authority schools), 'and secondly that the scholars shall not have imposed on them teachers who are out of harmony with the principles of their parents'. As a result, at the primary level, nearly all Catholic schools remained voluntary schools, and nearly all local authority schools, though ostensibly non-denominational, became in effect schools for Protestant children, staffed by Protestant teachers and providing religious education acceptable to the Protestant churches.[6] Again, in 1947, when education in Northern Ireland was re-organised, the 50 per cent grant for buildings and equipment which the government gave to voluntary (and therefore Catholic) schools was raised to 65 per cent, but the proposal aroused so much opposition that – though the grant *was* raised – the Minister of Education, Colonel Hall-Thompson, was later forced to resign. His colleague Mr William Grant, the Minister of Health, however refused to allow the Mater Infirmorum Hospital in Belfast, which was a Catholic institution practising Catholic medical principles (and which therefore wished to remain outside the National Health Service) to receive government grants. 'They are either coming in 100 per cent, or they are staying out 100 per cent', he declared. 'There is going to be no half-way stage about this matter.' The hospital consequently remained outside the Health Service until 1 January 1972.

In the end the problem in Northern Ireland is one of two minorities – a Catholic minority which has a traditional loyalty to a united Ireland, and a Protestant majority, which would become a minority in such a united Ireland. Because of what it believes to be discrimination against the Protestant minority in the Republic, the Protestant majority in Northern Ireland has behaved as if it were a besieged minority. Because of the discrimination that this siege mentality has caused, the Catholic minority in Northern Ireland have become obsessed with their minority position. Though many of the grievances raised in the Civil Rights movement of the mid-1960s have now been remedied, it will be a long time before this shows itself in any general improvement in the status and well-being of the hitherto deprived Catholic minority, concentrated in any case at the lower end of the social and economic scale and living very largely in city ghettos like Ballymurphy and the Bogside. Unless a genuinely open and pluralistic society can be created in Ireland which is concerned with the rights of people, not as Roman Catholics or Protestants, but simply as *people*, neither Roman Catholics nor Protestants can be relieved of the fundamental anxieties about their identity and their future.

[5] A system of secular education would in fact have been equally unacceptable to Catholics, but they took no part in the campaign against the Act.

[6] The division is much less complete at the secondary level, though it is still important.

BIBLIOGRAPHY

This list mentions some of the most recent and more easily available books, in many of which there are also more detailed bibliographies.

GENERAL WORKS

BECKETT, J. C. *A short history of Ireland* Hutchinson, 4th edn, cased and paperback 1972.

BECKETT, J. C. *The making of modern Ireland, 1603–1923* Faber, 1966; paperback n.e. 1969.

CULLEN, L. M. *An economic history of Ireland since 1660* Batsford, 1972.

CULLEN, L. M. ed. *The formation of the Irish economy* Cork: Mercier Press, paperback 1968.

CULLEN, L. M. *Life in Ireland* Batsford, 1968. o.p.

JOHNSTON, E. M. *Irish history : a select bibliography* Historical Assoc., rev. edn. paperback 1972.

LYONS, F. S. L. *Ireland since the Famine* Weidenfeld and Nicolson, 1971; Fontana, rev. edn. 1973.

MACDONAGH, O. *Ireland* Prentice-Hall, cased and paperback 1968.

MAGEE, J. *The teaching of Irish history in Irish Schools* Northern Ireland Community Relations Commission, 16 Bedford St., Belfast BT2 7FD, paperback 1972.

MOODY, T. W. and MARTIN, F. X. eds. *The course of Irish history* Cork: Mercier Press, cased and paperback 1967.

MOODY, T. W. ed. *Irish historiography, 1936–70* Dublin: Irish Committee of Historical Sciences, 40 Trinity College, 1972.

NORMAN, E. R. *A history of modern Ireland* Allen Lane, 1971; Penguin Books, 1973.

O'BRIEN, C. C. and M. A. *A concise history of Ireland* Thames and Hudson, 1972.

ZIMMERMAN, G. D. *Songs of the Irish rebellion : political street ballads and rebel songs, 1780–1900* Hatboro. Pa; Folklore Assoc., 1967.

CHAPTER ONE: REMEMBER 1690!

BECKETT, J. C. *Protestant dissent in Ireland, 1687–1780* Faber, 1948. o.p.

BOLTON, G. C. *The passing of the Irish Act of Union* O.U.P., 1966.

CLARKE, A. *The Old English in Ireland, 1625–42* MacGibbon and Kee, 1966, o.p.

JAMES, F. G. *Ireland in the Empire 1688–1770* Harvard University Press, 1973.

JOHNSTON, E. M. *Great Britain and Ireland, 1760–1800* Oliver and Boyd, 1963.

KEARNEY, H. F. *Strafford in Ireland, 1633–41* Manchester University Press, 1960.

MACCURTAIN, M. *Tudor and Stuart Ireland* Dublin: Gill and Macmillan, paperback 1972.

MACLYSAGHT, E. *Irish life in the seventeenth century* Irish University Press, 3rd edn. 1970.

MAXWELL, C. *Country and town in Ireland under the Georges* Dundalk: Dundalgan Press, n.e. 1949. o.p.

MAXWELL, C. *Dublin under the Georges* Faber, 1956. o.p.

MOODY, T. W. *The Londonderry Plantation, 1609–41* Belfast: W. Mullen, 1939. o.p.

OTWAY-RUTHVEN, A. J. *A history of mediaeval Ireland* Benn, 1968.

PAKENHAM, T. *The year of liberty : the story of the great Irish Rebellion of 1798* Hodder and Stoughton, 1969; Panther, 1972.

PUBLIC RECORD OFFICE *Aspects of Irish social history, 1750–1800* ed. by W. M. Crawford and B. Trainor. Belfast: HMSO, 1969.

SENIOR, H. *Orangeism in Ireland and Britain, 1795–1836* Routledge and Kegan Paul, 1966.

SIMMS, J. G. *The Williamite confiscation in Ireland, 1690–1703* Faber, 1956. o.p.

WALL, M. *The penal laws 1691–1760* Dundalk: Dundalgan Press for the Dublin Historical Association, 1961.

CHAPTER TWO: THE LAND FOR THE PEOPLE

ARENSBERG, C. M. and KIMBALL, S. T. *Family and community in Ireland* Harvard University Press, 2nd edn. 1968.

BLACK, R. D. C. *Economic thought and the Irish question, 1817–1870* C.U.P., 1960. o.p.

CONNELL, K. H. *The population of Ireland, 1750–1845* O.U.P., 1950.

CONNELL, K. H. *Irish peasant society* O.U.P., 1968.

EDWARDS, R. D. and WILLIAMS, T. D. eds. *The Great Famine* Dublin: Browne and Nolan, 1957. No longer publishing.

FREEMAN, T. W. *Pre-famine Ireland : a study in historical geography* Manchester University Press, 1957.

POMFRET, J. E. *The struggle for land in Ireland, 1800–1923* Princeton U.P., and O.U.P., 1930; reprinted by Russell, New York, 1969.

SCHRIER, A. *Ireland and the American emigration, 1850–1900* Minnesota University Press, 1958; reprinted by Russell, New York, 1970.

SOLOW, B. *The land question and the Irish economy, 1870–1903* Harvard University Press, 1972.

WOODHAM-SMITH, C. *The Great Hunger* Hamish Hamilton, 1962; New English Library, 1970.

CHAPTER THREE: GOD SAVE IRELAND!

CURTIS, L. P. *Apes and angels: Irishman in Victorian carica-ture* David and Charles, 1971.

CURTIS, L. P. *Coercion and conciliation in Ireland, 1880–92* Princeton University Press, 1963.

KEE, R. *The green flag: a history of Irish nationalism* Weidenfeld and Nicolson, 1972.

LEE, J. *The modernization of Irish society, 1848–1918* Dublin: Gill and Macmillan, paperback 1973.

LYONS, F. S. L. *The fall of Parnell, 1890–91* Routledge and Kegan Paul, 1960.

LYONS, F. S. L. *Parnell* Dundalk: W. Tempest for the Dublin Historical Association, paperback 1963.

MACINTYRE, A. *The Liberator: Daniel O'Connell and the Irish Party, 1830–1847* Hamish Hamilton, 1965. o.p.

MANSERGH, N. *The Irish question, 1840–1921* George Allen and Unwin, 1965. o.p.; paperback 1969.

O'BRIEN, C. C. *Parnell and his Party, 1880–90* O.U.P., 1957.

O'HEGARTY, P. S. *A history of Ireland under the Union, 1801–1922* Methuen, 1952. o.p.

O'TUATHAIGH, G. *Ireland before the famine, 1789–1848* Dublin: Gill and Macmillan, paperback 1972.

REYNOLDS, J. A. *The Catholic emancipation crisis in Ireland, 1823–1829* Yale University Press, 1954; O.U.P., 1955. o.p.

CHAPTER FOUR: ULSTER WILL FIGHT

BARKLEY, J. M. *St. Enoch's congregation, 1872–1972: an account of Presbyterianism in Belfast through the life of a congregation* The Secretary, St. Enoch's Church, Carlisle Circus, Belfast. paperback 1972.

BECKETT, J. C. and GLASSCOCK, R. E. eds. *Belfast: the origin and growth of an industrial city* BBC, 1967.

BOYD, A. *Holy war in Belfast* Tralee: Anvil Books, paper-back 1969.

BUCKLAND, P. J. *Irish unionism* 2 vols. Dublin: Gill and Macmillan, 1973. Vol. 1. *The Anglo-Irish and the new Ireland, 1885–1922*. Vol. 2. *Ulster unionism and the origins of Northern Ireland, 1886–1922*.

BUCKLAND, P. J. *Irish unionism, 1885–1922. A documentary history* Belfast: HMSO, 1973.

BUCKLAND, P. J. *Irish unionism* Historical Assoc., paper-back 1973.

COE, W. E. *The engineering industry of the north of Ireland* David and Charles, 1969.

de PAOR, L. *Divided Ulster* Penguin Books, 2nd edn. 1971.

GILL, C. *The rise of the Irish linen industry* O.U.P., 1925, reprinted 1964.

GREEN, E. R. R. *The Lagan Valley, 1800–50: a local history of the Industrial Revolution* Faber, 1949.

JONES, E. *A social geography of Belfast* O.U.P., 1960. o.p.

MOODY, T. W. and BECKETT, J. C. eds. *Ulster since 1800: a political and economic survey* BBC, 1955. o.p.

MOODY, T. W. and others *Ulster since 1800: a social survey* BBC, 1957. o.p.

STEWART, A. T. Q. *The Ulster Crisis* Faber, 1967. o.p., paperback 1970.

CHAPTER FIVE: GREEN, WHITE AND GOLD

BOYCE, D. G. *Englishmen and Irish troubles: British public opinion and the making of Irish policy, 1918–22* Cape, 1972.

BYRNE, F. J. and MARTIN, F. X. eds. *Eoin MacNeill and the making of the new Ireland* Irish University Press, 1973.

CAULFIELD, M. *The Easter Rebellion* Muller, 1964. o.p.; New English Library, 1965. o.p.

GREAVES, C. D. *Life and time of James Connolly* Lawrence and Wishart, 2nd rev. edn. 1972.

HOLT, E. *Protest in arms: the Irish troubles, 1916–23* Put-nam, 1960. o.p.

INGLIS, B. *Roger Casement* Hodder and Stoughton, 1973.

LYONS, F. S. L. *The Irish Parliamentary Party, 1890–1910* Faber, 1951. o.p.

LYONS, F. S. L. *John Dillon* Routledge and Kegan Paul, 1968.

MARTIN, F. X. ed. *Leaders and men of the Easter Rising: Dublin 1916* (RTE, Thomas Davis lectures) Methuen, 1967. o.p.

NOWLAN, K. B. *The making of 1916* The Stationery Office, Dublin, 1969.

O'BRIEN, C. C. *The shaping of modern Ireland* Routledge and Kegan Paul, cased and paperback 1960.

THOMPSON, W. I. *The imagination of an insurrection. Dublin, Easter 1916* O.U.P., 1967. o.p; Harper and Row, paperback 1972.

WILLIAMS, D. ed. *The Irish struggle, 1916–26* Routledge and Kegan Paul, 1966.

CHAPTER SIX: FREEDOM TO ACHIEVE FREEDOM

BOWYER BELL, J. *The secret army: a history of the IRA, 1916–70* Blond, 1970; Sphere, 1972.

CHUBB, B. *The government and politics of Ireland* O.U.P., 1970.

COOGAN, T. P. *Ireland since the rising* Pall Mall Press, 1966. o.p.

COOGAN, T. P. *The IRA* Pall Mall Press, 1970; Fontana, 1971.

HARKNESS, D. W. *The restless dominion: the Irish Free State and the British Commonwealth of Nations, 1921–31* Macmillan, 1969.

IRISH BOUNDARY COMMISSION *Report of the Irish Boundary Commission, 1925* edited by G. J. Hand. Irish University Press, 1969.

JONES, T. *Whitehall diary* vol. 3 *Ireland 1918–25* edited by K. Middlemas. O.U.P., 1971.

MANNING, M. *Irish political parties: an introduction* Dublin: Gill and Macmillan, paperback 1972.

PAKENHAM, F. (now Earl of Longford) *Peace by ordeal: the negotiation and signature of the Anglo-Irish Treasury, 1921* Cape, 1935. o.p; Sidgwick and Jackson n.e. cased and paperback 1972.

PAKENHAM, F. (now Earl of Longford) and O'NEILL, T. P. *Eamon de Valera* Hutchinson, 1970.

YOUNGER, C. *Ireland's civil war* Muller, 1968; Fontana, 1970.

CHAPTER SEVEN: WHAT WE HAVE WE HOLD

BARRITT, D. P. and CARTER, C. F. *The Northern Ireland problem* O.U.P., 2nd edn. paperback 1972.

ERVINE, ST. J. *Craigavon: Ulsterman* George Allen and Unwin, 1949. o.p.

HARRIS, R. *Prejudice and tolerance in Ulster: a study of neighbours and 'strangers' in a border community* Manchester University Press, 1972.

HESLINGA, M. W. *The Irish border as a cultural divide* Humanities Press, 2nd edn. cased and paperback 1972.

LAWRENCE, R. J. *The government of Northern Ireland: public finance and public services, 1921–1964* O.U.P., 1965.

O'NEILL, Baron *The autobiography of Terence O'Neill* Hart-Davis, 1972.

ROSE, R. *Governing without concensus: an Irish perspective* Faber, 1971.

WALLACE, M. *Northern Ireland: fifty years of self-government* David and Charles, 1971.

WILSON, T. ed. *Ulster under Home Rule* O.U.P., 1955. o.p. *Disturbances in Northern Ireland: Report of the Cameron Commission* (Cmd 532) Belfast: HMSO, 1969.

CHAPTER EIGHT: WHEN THE BOUGH BREAKS

CROTTY, R. D. *Irish agricultural production: its volume and structure* Cork University Press, 1966.

CUTHBERT, N. and ISLES, K. S. *An economic survey of Northern Ireland* Belfast: HMSO, 1957.

FITZGERALD, G. M. *Planning in Ireland* Dublin: Institute of Public Administration, 1969.

FITZGERALD, G. M. *State-sponsored bodies* Dublin: Institute of Public Administration, 2nd edn. 1963.

HEALEY, J. *The death of an Irish town* Cork: Mercier Press, 2nd edn. paperback 1968.

MEENAN, J. *The Irish economy since 1922* Liverpool University Press, 1970.

MOGEY, J. M. *Rural life in Northern Ireland* O.U.P., 1947. o.p.

Economic development (Pr 4803) Dublin: Stationery Office, 1958.

Report of the Joint Working Party on the economy of Northern Ireland (Chairman: Sir Robert Hall) (Cmd 446) Belfast: HMSO, 1962.

Economic development in Northern Ireland (Chairman: Prof. Thomas Wilson) (Cmd 479) Belfast: HMSO, 1964.

Report of the Commission on Emigration and other Population Problems, 1948–54 (Pr 2541) Dublin: Stationery Office, 1956.

CHAPTER NINE: THIS HANDFUL OF DREAMS

BOYD, E. A. *Ireland's literary renaissance* Figgis, n.e. 1969.

BRODY, H. *Inishkillane: change and decline in the west of Ireland* Allen Lane, 1973.

BROWN, M. *The politics of Irish literature: from Thomas Davis to W. B. Yeats* George Allen and Unwin, 1972.

DONOGHUE, D. *Yeats* Fontana, 1971.

ELLIS-FERMOR, U. *The Irish dramatic movement* Methuen, paperback 1967.

HOWARTH, H. *The Irish writers, 1880–1940: literature under Parnell's star* Rockliff, 1958. o.p.

O'CUIV, B. ed. *A view of the Irish language* Dublin: Stationery Office, 1969.

SKELTON, R. *The writings of J. M. Synge* Thames and Hudson, 1971.

SOMERVILLE, E. A. O. and ROSS, M. *The real Charlotte* Zodiac Press, 1972.

SYNGE, J. M. *Collected works* 4 vols. O.U.P., 1962–68.

USSHER, A. *The face and mind of Ireland* Gollancz, 1949. o.p.

YEATS, W. B. *Collected poems* Macmillan, 2nd edn. 1950. *Commission on the restoration of the Irish language. Summary in English, of the Final Report* (Pr 7256) Dublin: Stationery Office, 1963.

The restoration of the Irish language: Government White Paper (Pr 8061) Dublin: Stationery Office, 1965.

CHAPTER TEN: HOME RULE IS ROME RULE

AKENSON, D. *Education and enmity: the control of schooling in Northern Ireland, 1920–50* David and Charles, 1973.

BARKLEY, J. M. *A short history of the Presbyterian Church in Ireland* Presbyterian Church in Ireland, 1959.

BLANCHARD, J. *The church in contemporary Ireland* Burns and Oates, 1964. No longer publishing.

HURLEY, M. ed. *Irish Anglicism, 1869–1969* Figgis, 1970.

JACKSON, H. *The two Irelands: the problem of the double minority – a dual study of inter-group tensions* Minority Rights Group, n.e. 1972.

NORMAN, E. R. *The Catholic Church and Ireland in the age of rebellion, 1859–73* Longman, 1965.

VINEY, M. *The five per cent: a survey of Protestants in the Republic.* Dublin: *Irish Times,* 1966.

WHYTE, J. H. *Church and state in modern Ireland, 1923–1970* Dublin: Gill and Macmillan, 1971.

INDEX